THE
BAYEUX TAPESTRY

The Battle of Hastings and the Norman Conquest

JOHN COLLINGWOOD BRUCE,

". . . They burning both with fervent fire
Their countrey's auncestry to understond."

Spenser

DORSET PRESS
New York

This edition published by Dorset Press,
a division of Marboro Books Corporation,
by arrangement with Bestseller Publications Ltd.

First published 1856
by John Russell Smith, London.
Colour plates reproduced from *La Tapisserie de Bayeux*
Edition Variorum, illustrated by Victor Sansonetti.
Paris, 1838

ISBN 0-88029-153-2

Printed and bound in Singapore.

CONTENTS

LIST OF ILLUSTRATIONS

Between pages 38 and 39:

THE

BAYEUX TAPESTRY.

I. THE ROLL.

" There she weaves, by night and day,
A magic web with colours gay."
Tennyson.

MASTER WACE, to whom we are indebted for " the most minute,
graphic, and animated account of the transactions "[a] of the Norman Conquest, thus exalts the art of the chronicler—" All things
hasten to decay; all fall; all perish; all come to an end.
Man dieth, iron consumeth, wood decayeth; towers crumble,
strong walls fall down, the rose withereth away; the war-horse
waxeth feeble, gay trappings grow old; all the works of men
perish.   Thus we are taught that all die, both clerk and lay; and
short would be the fame of any after death if their history did not
endure by being written in the book of the clerk."[b]

The pen of the writer of romance is not the only implement
which confers immortality upon man.   The chisel of the sculptor,
the pencil of the painter, and the needle of the high-born dame,
can confer a lasting renown upon those whose deeds are worthy of

[a] Taylor's Wace, p. xv.   [b] Ibid. p. 3.

B

being remembered.   The work which we are about to consider was effected by the simplest of these implements—the needle.

One of the earliest modes of transmitting the history of important transactions to posterity was by recording them in long lines of pictorial representation.   In the temples of Nimroud, in the sepulchres of Egypt, in the sculptures which entwine the columns of Trajan and Antonine at Rome, we have familiar examples of the practice.   The Bayeux record is a large roll of historic drawings rather than a piece of tapestry; and it is remarkable as being the last example of this species of representation which antiquity has handed down to us.

In the days of the Conqueror, and of some of his Saxon predecessors, the ladies of Engle-land were famous for their taste and skill in embroidery; and this species of lady-like manufacture was known throughout Europe as English work.[a]

One effect of the Conquest was to bring the people of England and Normandy into closer alliance than before.   On the first occasion on which William returned to Normandy, after the battle of Hastings, he took with him, "in honourable attendance," a considerable number of the Saxon nobles,[b] who were doubtless accompanied by their wives and daughters.   Assisted by English ladies, as well as by those of her own court, Matilda, the wife of the Conqueror, probably at this time constructed the Tapestry which for many ages was preserved in the Cathedral of Bayeux.

Never, perhaps, was so important a document written in worsted.

[a] Archæologia, vol. xvii., p. 105.   [b] Ordericus Vitalis, bk. iv., ch. ii.

It is a full and a faithful chronicle of an event on which the modern history of the world has turned. It is referred to as an historical authority by nearly every writer who discusses the period. The way in which the subject is treated, the spirit shown in its design, and the harmony of its colouring, warrant us in pronouncing it to be a monument worthy of its reputed author, and of the event which it is designed to commemorate.

It is, however, a double memorial; it is a record of the love and duty of William's consort, as well as of the skill and valour of the great hero himself. A loving wife sympathizes with her husband in all his tastes. She takes an enthusiastic interest in his favourite pursuits; and she had "lever far," to use an expression of Lady Payson's, that success attended his efforts—that another leaf were added to his laurel crown—"than that she should have a new gown, though it were of scarlet." Matilda could not bestride the war-horse, and do battle in the field by her husband's side; but she could commit his exploits to the Tapestry. Surrounded by her ladies, all adroitly using their many-coloured threads, she—

> Fought all his battles o'er again;
> And thrice [she] routed all his foes, and thrice [she] slew the slain.

Matilda was, during the greater part of her life, a loving wife. William, too, was a devoted and faithful husband; though in one case he cannot be recommended as a model to enamoured swains. It is said that for seven long years he courted Matilda of Flanders, but in vain. Her affections were set upon a Saxon nobleman, but were not reciprocated. At length the Duke resolved to bring matters to a crisis. He repaired to Bruges, and met the high-bred damsel as she returned from church through the streets of her father's gay capital. Having reproached her for her long-continued scorn and cruelty, he seized her, and coolly rolled her in the mud, to the no small injury of her trim and costly attire. Then, after a few more striking proofs of his regard, which she must have sensibly felt from such a hand, the lover rode away at full speed, leaving her to account for this novel mode of courtship as best she could. Strangely enough, she put a charitable construction upon his actions; she regarded his blows as so many proofs of the violence of his affection; she felt sorry for him; and then—all was over—in a very brief space the nuptial ceremonies were solemnized with a splendour becoming the greatness of the occasion.[a]

Thus did William win the hand of a lady who was to give to England a race of monarchs more renowned than those of any other dynasty. She herself, let it be observed, had the blood of Alfred in her veins.

Before proceeding further, it may be well to give a brief reply to the question which will naturally arise in the minds of most— Has the Bayeux Tapestry descended to us from a period so remote as that of the Conquest? A minute examination of the work supplies the best answer to this question. Montfaucon, whose knowledge of antiquities no one will dispute, and who was the

[a] Roscoe's Life of the Conqueror, p. 92. *See* Note A. at the end of the volume.

first to describe the Tapestry as a whole, was quite satisfied that popular tradition was correct in ascribing it to the wife of the Conqueror; and Thierry, the last and ablest writer upon the Norman Conquest, though he hesitates to ascribe the work to Matilda, has no doubt that it is contemporaneous with the Conquest, and constantly refers to it as a document of unquestionable authenticity.[a]

Not, however, to settle the question by authorities, it may be observed :—1st. That the fulness and correctness of its historical details prove that it is a contemporaneous chronicle. Wace, as has already been observed, treats more largely of the Norman invasion than any of the writers of the Norman period ; and, such is the general agreement between the verses of the one and the delineations of the other, that the Tapestry may be pronounced to be what in these latter days would be called the " illustrations," and the narrative of the chronicler the " letter-press," of an elaborate history of the Norman Conquest.[b] And yet the one does not follow the other slavishly. Whilst they agree in all the general facts, they differ in many minute details, as all independent narratives will.

2. Again, the architecture, the dresses, the armour, the furniture, of the Tapestry are those which prevailed at the period of the Conquest, and at no other. It is at all times exceedingly difficult, whether by writing or painting, to portray accurately the manners, language, and modes of thought, of an anterior period. In mediæval times, however, the attempt was seldom made. The

[a] *See* Note B. at the end of the volume. [b] Taylor's Wace, p. xxviii.

draftsmen represented the manners "living as they rose."
"It was the invariable practice with artists in every country,"
says Mr. Charles Stothard,[a] "excepting Italy, during the middle
ages, whatever subject they took in hand, to represent it according to the manners and customs of their own time. Thus we may
see Alexander the Great, like a good Catholic, interred with all
the rites and ceremonies of the Romish church. All the illuminated transcripts of Froissart, although executed not more than
fifty years after the original work was finished, are less valuable
on account of the illuminations they contain not being accordant
with the text, but representing the customs of the fifteenth
century instead of the fourteenth. It is not likely that in an age
far less refined this practice should be departed from. The
Tapestry, therefore, must be regarded as a true picture of the time
when it was executed." The testimony of an earlier authority,
Strutt, is to the same effect :—" To a total want of proper taste in
collecting of antiquities, and application to the study of them, are
owing the ignorant errors committed by the unlearned illuminators
of old MSS. ; and so far were they from having the least idea of
any thing more ancient than the manners and customs of their
own particular times, that not only things of a century earlier than
their own era, are confounded together, but even representations
of the remotest periods in history. The Saxons put Noah, Abra-
ham, Christ, and King Edgar, all in the same habit, that is, the
habit worn by themselves at that time ; and in some MSS., illu-

[a] Archæologia, vol. xix., p. 186.

minated in the reign of Henry the Sixth, are exhibited the figures of Meleager, Hercules, Jason, &c., in the full dress of the great lords of that prince's court. At the latter end of one of these MSS., indeed, the illuminator, reading something about a lion's skin, has covered the shoulders of the beau Hercules with that kingly animal's hide over his courtly load of silk and gold embroidery. Yet this is a lucky circumstance in the present want of ancient materials; for though these pictures do not bear the least resemblance of the things they were originally intended to represent, yet they nevertheless are the undoubted characteristics of the customs of that period in which each illuminator or designer lived."[a] A comparison of Master Wace with the Bayeux Tapestry will furnish us with an illustration in point. Wace, after alluding to the negotiations which took place before the armies closed at the decisive field of Hastings, says, " As the Duke said this, and would have said more, William Fitz Osbern rode up, *his horse all covered*

[a] Strutt thus disposes of a difficulty which may occur to some minds.—" If any one should say, by way of objection to this established rule, that though the illuminator has not given us the customs, habits, &c., of those people he designed to picture out, yet is it not most likely that such dresses as are given should be fictitious, agreeable rather to his own wild fancy than to the real customs and habits of his own times? To answer their objection, (and that because the chief materials of the present work are collected from the ancient MSS.) the reader must be informed, that many of these MSS. (especially such as are illuminated) were done as presents, or at the command of kings and noblemen, who are generally represented in the frontispiece in their proper habits receiving the particular MS. done for them from the author, and they are generally pictured attended by their court, or retinue. That these figures should be habited in the true dress of the times will not be doubted; and then, as far as the anonymous illuminations which may chance to follow in the MS. shall agree with those figures in the frontispiece, so far they may

with iron; Sire, said he to his lord, we tarry too long, let us arm
ourselves. Allons! Allons!"[a] Now, if we look at the Tapestry,
we shall find that not a single horse is equipped in steel armour; and
if we refer to the authors who lived at that period, we shall find
that not one of them mentions any defensive covering for the horse.
Wace, who flourished in the days of Henry I. and Henry II., is the
first writer who mentions horse-armour, and, excepting from the
passage which has just been quoted, it could not be proved that it
had been introduced even in his day. Wace is therefore probably
guilty of an anachronism, and describes what happened at the close
of his own time as having occurred in that of his immediate predecessors.[b] This example shows how exceedingly difficult it is to
portray customs with accuracy a few years after the period in
which they prevailed. Had the Tapestry been made by Matilda
the Empress, as some contend, numerous similar anachronisms
must have occurred.

be allowed as authentic; other MSS. were done for particular abbeys and monasteries, in the embellishments of which no pains were spared. But a still greater
proof of the authenticity of these delineations is, that on examining all the illuminated MSS. of the same century together, which, tho' various, every one written and
ornamented by different hands, yet on comparing the several delineations with each
other, they will be found to agree in every particular of dress, customs, &c., even in
the minutiæ, which perfect similitude it would have been impossible to have
preserved, had not some sure standard been regularly taken for the whole; therefore
the fancy of the painter will be found to have little share in these valuable
delineations. Besides, these pictures constantly agree with the description of the
habits and customs of the same period, collected from the old historians."—*Strutt's
Manners, Customs, &c., of the Inhabitants of England*, vol. i, p. 3.

[a] Taylor's Wace, p. 162.   [b] Ibid. p. 163. *n.*

3. But the design of the Tapestry shows its early date. Its manifest object is to prove the right of William to the throne of England, to exhibit in strong colours the undutifulness and ingratitude of Harold in attempting the usurpation of the crown, and to record the punishment with which that disloyal and sacrilegious act was visited.[a] In the latter days of the Conqueror such an undertaking would have been valueless. He had planted his foot firmly upon the necks of the native population; the barons, too, by whom he achieved the Conquest, had been brought into subjection. He was king of England by the power of his sword; he cared not then about the will of Edward the Confessor, the oath of Harold, or the election of the nobles—he was king *de facto*, and let them who durst deny it! These remarks, made with reference to the close of the Conqueror's reign, apply with still greater force to the time of the Empress Matilda, to whom, as some conceive, we are indebted for the Tapestry.[b] She would not have thought it necessary to establish in so elaborate a manner her deceased grandfather's right to the throne, and to display at such length the obligations under

[a] "All have hitherto treated the Bayeux Tapestry as a 'Monument of the Conquest of England,' following therein M. Lancelot, and speaking of it as an unfinished work: whereas it is an apologetical history of the claims of William to the crown of England, and of the breach of faith, and fall of Harold; and is a perfect and finished action."—*Mr. Hudson Gurney*, Archæologia, vol. xvii., p. 361.

[b] The Abbé de la Rue, in an elaborate paper in the *Archæologia* (vol. xvii, p. 85-109), supports the opinion that the Tapestry was prepared at the command of Matilda, daughter of Henry I. and wife of Henry V. Emperor of Germany. Lord Lyttleton (History of Henry II., vol. i, p. 353) and Hume (History of England, vol. i, *note* F.) entertain similar views.

C

which Harold lay to him. The Brittany campaign would not have been given in such detail excepting it had been quite a recent event. The Tapestry, it will be observed, ends with the battle of Hastings. It does not even include the subsequent coronation of William. It represents the first act in the drama of the Conquest of England, and was doubtless intended to prepare for the scenes which were to follow. It is difficult to conceive that the Tapestry was designed at any period save that immediately subsequent to the battle of Hastings. William had not then assumed the character of an arbitrary monarch, which he subsequently did. The Saxon ladies, full of reverence for the character of their lately deceased monarch, Edward the Confessor, might naturally resent the attempt of Harold to resist the evident wish of that monarch to bequeath his crown to William, and, imbued with the superstition of an ignorant age, regard the fatal results of the battle of Hastings as a just judgment from God for the violation of an oath taken upon the relics of the saints. Taking this view of it there was nothing unpatriotic in their entering zealously into the views of their queen. But if, after England had reaped the bitter fruits of the conquest; if, after their fathers had been slain, their husbands driven into exile, their children made to herd with the dogs of the Conqueror's flock, they had lent their skill to commemorate the desolation of their country and their homes, they would have dishonoured their lineage and their name. On these general grounds, therefore, we may conceive the Tapestry to be of the era of the Conqueror, and to date from an early period in his reign. Many opportunities of reverting to this subject will afterwards occur.

But although it be admitted that the Tapestry is of the age of the Conquest, it does not necessarily follow that it was wrought by the Queen and her court. The opinion that Matilda presided over its execution has been strongly controverted, chiefly by those, however, who deny its early antiquity. The Abbé de la Rue, as formerly observed, ascribes it to Matilda the Empress. Mr. Bolton Corney, in an able paper entitled *Researches and Conjectures on the Bayeux Tapestry*, contends that it was not executed until the year 1205, and that it was then done at the expense of the Chapter. Dr. Lingard adopts Mr. Corney's views, and in a note appended to the first volume of his *History of England* condenses his arguments. If, however, the Tapestry bear internal evidence of an earlier date, these arguments are of little value.

No contemporary historian indeed tells us that the Tapestry was made by Matilda. It is not mentioned in her will, or the Conqueror's. The inventory of the treasures of the church at Bayeux, bearing date 1369, and which is the earliest document mentioning the Tapestry, contains no allusion to Matilda. Another inventory, made in 1476, and professing to be a descriptive catalogue of the jewels, ornaments, books, and other valuables of the church, mentions the Tapestry, describes its form and subject, and names the period of its public exhibition; but gives no hint that it was made at the command of Matilda. It is difficult, it may even be impossible, satisfactorily to account for the absence of all allusion to the Queen in these documents, but negative arguments prove little. Besides, the case is by no means singular. The compilers of ancient documents seem to have left much to be taken for granted. Sir Henry Ellis, in his *General Introduction to Domesday*, says, " Of Queen Matilda's gifts to foreign monasteries, two only are particularly specified in the Survey; the land at Deverel in Wilts, which she gave to St. Mary at Bec; and two hides at Frantone in Dorset, which she gave to the Conqueror's foundation of St. Stephen at Caen. *No mention occurs of the Conqueror and his Queen having founded the monasteries of St. Stephen and the Holy Trinity in that city:* although their lands in England are specified."[a] It is scarcely less difficult to account for these omissions in the *Domesday Book*, than it is to account for the absence of all allusion to the framer of the Tapestry by contemporary writers. In the absence of direct evidence, we are thrown upon probabilities. And what is more likely than that the opinion which Montfaucon found prevailing at Bayeux when he discovered the Tapestry is the correct one? As the Abbé de la Rue himself argues, " To have undertaken this Tapestry would have required a considerable degree of interest in the subject of it, and to have possessed the necessary powers for its execution."[b] Who can be supposed to have had so great an interest in the establishment of the Conqueror's right to the throne of England as Matilda of Flanders, and who but herself would have been at the trouble of asserting it in such full detail? Would any one but an immediate connexion of the Duke's have taken such prominent notice of the

[a] Vol. i., p. 328, 8vo. edition.   [b] Archæologia, vol. xvii., p. 105.

rescue of Harold from his captivity in Ponthieu, and of his subsequent friendly intercourse with William in Brittany; and would even Matilda herself have done this if the Tapestry had been prepared after the stupendous results of the battle of Hastings had fully developed themselves?

Dr. Lingard, in appealing to the roll itself, says, " Nor does the costliness of the work bespeak a royal benefactor." " There is in it no embroidery of gold, none of silver, none of silk, nothing worthy the rank or the munificence of the supposed donor." Had the article in question been a royal robe, or sacerdotal vestment, the omission of the precious metals might have been unaccountable; but in a piece of embroidery of such extent, it is nothing wonderful. Neither should the artistic value of the document be overlooked. Its figures may appear uncouth in our eyes, but they are done in the very best style of the period. A person of ordinary resources could not have commanded, to the extent required, the services of the ablest artists of the day. The preparation of the Tapestry must have been a costly and laborious process, not at all unworthy of the wife of the victor of Hastings.[a] What is more likely, then, than that the traditional opinion which Montfaucon found prevailing in his day at Bayeux is well founded, and that to the first of our Norman Queens we are indebted for this most wonderful piece of needle-work?

[a] Some idea of the labour involved in the work may be learned from the number of figures represented in it. It contains 623 men, 202 horses, 55 dogs, 505 animals of various kinds not already enumerated, 37 buildings, 41 ships and boats, and 49 trees—in all 1512 figures.

Although the actual execution of the Tapestry devolved upon the ladies of Matilda's court, there can be no doubt that they wrought from a design prepared by some draftsman. The priests were the principal artists of that day. The Latin inscriptions prove that in that part of their work, at least, the ladies had the assistance of some educated person. The name of the designer has not come down to us; unless indeed there be truth in the following statement made by Miss Agnes Strickland:—"This pictorial chronicle of her mighty consort's achievments appears to have been, in part at least, designed for Matilda by Turold, a dwarf artist, who moved by a natural desire of claiming his share in the celebrity which he foresaw would attach to the work, has cunningly introduced his own effigies and name,[a] thus authenticating the Norman tradition, that he was the person who illuminated the canvas with the proper outlines and colours."[b] Though ignorant of the individual who designed the Tapestry, the style of the work induces us to believe that the artist was an Italian. The postures into which many of the figures are thrown are not English or French, but Italian.[c] The cordiality subsisting at the time of the Conquest between the courts of Normandy and Rome, and the suc-

[a] See Plate IV.

[b] Queens of England, vol. i., p. 66, edition 1851. I have been unable to meet with any authority for this statement.

[c] In a short visit which I made to Italy in the winter of 1853-4, I paid some attention to this subject. I have seen a *vettorino*, when protesting that his exorbitant charge was a most reasonable one, throw himself into all the contortions exhibited in the Tapestry.

cessful exhibition of Norman prowess for some time previously on the plains of the Italian peninsula, sufficiently account for the introduction of the peculiarities of southern Europe into the Tapestry.

Perhaps, however, we have acted rashly in having ventured even thus cursorily to touch upon the antiquity of the Tapestry. Miss Agnes Strickland, who, in her *Lives of the Queens of England*, shows how vigorously she can wield the pen, is rather indignant that any one who is not learned in cross-stitch, should venture to discuss the subject. Before we argue, she wants to know if we can sew. She says, "With due deference to the judgment of the lords of the creation on all subjects connected with policy and science, we venture to think that our learned friends, the archæologists and antiquaries, would do well to direct their intellectual powers to more masculine objects of inquiry, and leave the question of the Bayeux Tapestry (with all other matters allied to needle-craft) to the decision of the ladies, to whose province it belongs. It is matter of doubt to us whether one, out of the many gentlemen who have disputed Matilda's claims to that work, if called upon to execute a copy of either of the figures on canvas, would know how to put in the first stitch."[a] Few of the rougher sex would like to be put to the *experimentum acus*, and therefore it may be as well at once to exercise the best part of valour, and beat a hasty retreat.

The attention of the learned world was first, in modern times,

[a] Lives of the Queens of England, edition 1853, p. 65. *n*.

called to the Bayeux Tapestry by M. Lancelot, who in 1724 found a drawing of a portion of it in the Cabinet of Antiquities at Paris. He was struck with its appearance, and at once pronounced it to be of the age of William the Conqueror, and intended to commemorate his exploits; but he was unable to conjecture whether the drawing represented a bass-relief, a piece of sculpture surrounding a choir of a church or a tomb, a painting in fresco or upon a glass window, or even, he adds, if it be a piece of tapestry. He conceived that the original would be found at Caen. In consequence of his suggestion, Father Montfaucon made diligent inquiries, and, after some trouble, found the Tapestry, not at Caen, but at Bayeux. He ascertained that it was there popularly ascribed to Queen Matilda.[a] M. Lancelot further informs us that it was ordinarily called in the country *La Toilette de Duc Guillaume*. At that period, and for long afterwards, it was kept in a side chapel of the cathedral, rolled upon a kind of winch, and was exposed to public view only once a year, on the festival of the relics (July 1), and during the octave. On these occasions it was hung up in the nave of the church, which it completely surrounded.

In the autumn of 1803, when Bonaparte, then First Consul of France, contemplated the invasion of England, the Tapestry was brought from its obscurity at Bayeux, and exhibited in

---

[a] His words are " L'opinion commune à Bayeux est que ce fut la reine Mathilde, femme de Guillaume-le-Conquérant, qui la fit faire. Cette opinion, qui passe pour une tradition dans le pays, n'a rien que de fort vraisemblable."—*Jubinal's Tapisserie de Bayeux*, p. 1.

the National Museum at Paris, where it remained some months. The First Consul himself went to see it, and affected to be struck with that particular part *(Plate XIII.)* which represents the appearance of a meteor presaging the defeat of Harold: affording an opportunity for the inference, that the meteor which had then been lately seen in the south of France was the prelude to a similar event. The exhibition was popular; so much so, that a small dramatic piece was got up at the Theatre du Vaudeville, entitled *La Tapisserie de la Reine Mathilde,* in which Matilda was represented passing her time with her women in embroidering the exploits of her husband, never leaving their work, except to put up prayers for his success.

At present the Tapestry is preserved in the town's library at Bayeux, where it is advantageously exposed to view by being extended in eight lengths from end to end of the room, and is at the same time protected from injury by being covered with glass.

The Tapestry has originally formed one piece, and measures two hundred and twenty-seven feet in length, by about twenty inches in breadth. The groundwork of it is a strip of rather fine linen cloth, which, through age, has assumed the tinge of brown holland. The stitches consist of lines of coloured worsted laid side by side, and bound down at intervals with cross fastenings; as is seen in the frontispiece, which represents a portion of the Tapestry of the original size. The parts intended to represent flesh (the face, hands, or naked legs of the men) are left untouched by the needle. Considering the age of the Tapestry, it is in a remarkably perfect

c

state.   The first portion of it is somewhat injured, and the last five yards of it are very much defaced.   The colours chiefly used by the fair artists are—dark and light blue, red, pink, yellow, buff, and dark and light green.   On examining this interesting relic, I was struck with nothing so much as the freshness of the colours; and can entirely subscribe to the words of Mr. Hudson Gurney, in the *Archæologia*, "the colours are as bright and distinct, and the letters of the superscriptions as legible, as if of yesterday."

Perspective and light and shade are wholly disregarded.   An effort is made, by varying the colours employed, to avoid the confusion arising from this circumstance: thus, while the leg of a horse which is nearest to the spectator is painted blue, the one more removed will be coloured red; or if the one be pink, the other may be a greenish yellow.   The colours, owing probably to the restricted extent of them at the command of Matilda, are employed somewhat fancifully, and we have horses exhibited to us of hues which, could they be realized in living specimens in Hyde Park now-a-days, would attract the envy and admiration of all beholders.   Notwithstanding the liberty thus taken, the harmony of the colouring is such, that persons may look at the Tapestry for some time without discovering that truth, in this particular, has been in any degree violated.   Mr. Dawson Turner remarks, that " in point of drawing, the figures are superior to the contemporary sculpture at St. George's and elsewhere; and the performance is not deficient in energy."[a]   As we examine the figures in detail, we

---

[a] Letters from Normandy, vol. i. p. 241.

shall have occasion to notice the spirit and the expression which the artist has infused into his work.

Besides the principal subject, which occupies the central portion of the Tapestry, there is an ornamental border at the top and bottom of the field, which is filled with a variety of representations. Here the artist has indulged in a considerable play of fancy. Figures of birds and beasts which certainly never came out of Noah's ark are admitted into this menagerie. Probably many of these forms represent the griffins, centaurs, and other fabulous creatures which occupy so conspicuous a place in the romances of the period. Others clearly represent animals, such as the camel and lion, with which the people of that age could not be very familiar, but which would, on that account, furnish subjects of thought and conversation all the more exciting.

In the lower border of the roll, near the beginning, are some representations of the fables of Æsop. There is the crow and the fox, the wolf and the lamb, the crane and the wolf, the eagle and the tortoise, and some others. Besides these subjects, we have many of the operations of husbandry, such as ploughing, sowing, and harrowing. The sports of the field are not neglected. One man is seen shooting birds with a sling. At this period the sling had quite gone into disuse as a weapon of war, but was probably long afterwards retained for the purposes of the sportsman. In one compartment, a man is seen fighting, sword in hand, with a bear that is chained to a tree. In another, the huntsman summons his dogs to the chase. In some portions of the Tapestry the border has an evident reference to the main subject of the piece; towards the end of the work the whole of the lower margin is filled with the bodies of the slain, thus forming it, as it were, the foreground of the general delineation.

The whole picture is divided into seventy-two compartments or scenes, which are generally separated from one another by trees, or what are intended to represent such. The artist, very modestly mistrusting his own powers, has usually affixed an inscription, in Latin, to each subject, the more fully to explain his intention. The letters, like the figures, are stitched in worsted, and are about an inch in length.

That the Tapestry should from a period beyond all record have belonged to the church of Bayeux is nothing surprising. Odo, the uterine brother of William, who rendered the Conqueror such efficient assistance in the battle of Hastings, and in the subsequent government of the kingdom, was archbishop of that place. Matilda may, with great propriety have given it to him in acknowledgement of his services, and he with equal probability, for he was very munificent to his church, may have given it to the Chapter. There is no other period at which it could with so much probability have come into the possession of the ecclesiastics of Bayeux as during the episcopate of Odo.[a]

[a] Ducarel, Appendix I., p. 3.

II. THE COMMISSION.

" All hail, Macbeth ! that shalt be king hereafter."
Macbeth.

VERY frequently the means which we adopt to secure our ends are those by which Providence designs to thwart them.

During that disastrous period when England was subject to the incessant depredations of the Danes, Ethelred II. contracted a marriage with Emma, a daughter of Richard I., Duke of Normandy. Ethelred's conduct to his wife proved that the match was not one of affection ; his object evidently was to obtain the assistance of the powerful house of Rollo in resisting the attacks of the Vikings of the north. Instead of doing this, the alliance resulted in arraying the Normans amongst the enemies of England. Alfred and Edward, the sons of Ethelred and Emma, found an asylum in the Norman court during the supremacy of Sweyn and Canute. At one time an expedition was in readiness to leave the shores of Normandy, with a view of placing by force a son of Ethelred on the throne of his father. William of Malmesbury, speaking of the two youths, says—" I find that their uncle Richard (II.) took no steps to restore them to their country ; on the contrary, he married his sister Emma to the enemy and the invader. Robert, however, whom we have so frequently before mentioned as having gone to Jerusalem, assembling a fleet and embarking soldiers, made ready an expedition, boasting that he would set the crown on the head of his grand-nephews; and doubtlessly he would have made good his assertion, had not, as we have heard from our ancestors, an adverse wind constantly opposed him: but assuredly this was by the hidden counsel of God, in whose disposal are the powers of all kingdoms. The remains of the vessels, decayed through length of time, were still to be seen at Rouen in our days."[a] Thus half a century before William the Conqueror set out upon his expedition, a Norman invasion loomed in the distance.

Whilst the ships of Robert were rotting in the harbour of Rouen, Alfred and Edward, the sons of Emma, were being trained up in the court of Normandy in those habits and feelings which eventually led to the assembling of an armament which adverse winds were not destined to baffle. Alfred visiting England, was barbarously murdered; the Norman chroniclers assert that the cruel deed was instigated by Godwin. At length, by the death of Hardicanute, a way was opened for Edward, afterwards styled the Confessor, to the throne of his father. He was, however, at the time of his accession, as Camden expresses it, thoroughly Frenchified. He could scarcely speak a word of English. His court was filled with Normans, who usurped most of the official dignities. When advancing years compelled the monarch to take some steps for securing a fitting successor to the throne, his mind reverted to the court of

[a] William of Malmesbury's English Chronicle (Bohn's edition), p. 196.

Normandy. His immediate heir, Edgar Atheling, was too feeble a youth to be placed, in such turbulent times, in so responsible a position. When the choice lay between Harold the Saxon and William the Norman, the Confessor's early predilictions necessarily induced him to look favourably upon the youthful head of his mother's house. Independently of any communications which the English king may have made to the young Duke of Normandy, the partiality which he manifested towards him could not fail to nurture in Duke William's mind the most ambitious views. Hence sprung the Norman invasion.

We are now prepared for examining in detail the scenes depicted in the Tapestry.

The first compartment exhibits to us Edward the Confessor giving audience to two personages of rank. The king is seated on a throne; his feet rest upon a footstool. A crown, ornamented with *fleurs-de-lis*, is on his head, and he holds a sceptre in his left hand. The robe of the monarch is full, and is ornamented at the collar, the wrists, and down the front, probably by needle-work of gold. Similar ornaments appear upon his knees. The arms and feet of the throne, according to the usage of the period, terminate in carvings of the head and feet of a dog. The taller of the persons waiting upon the king is no doubt Harold, as the face bears a strong resemblance to that of one of the horsemen in the next group, which the inscription tells us is Harold. A general likeness is preserved throughout the Tapestry, both in the case of William and Harold, so that we may reasonably suppose that the delineations of these personages bear some resemblance to the originals, and that they were drawn by an artist who knew them both. Edward is in the attitude of a king giving law to his subjects. Harold and his companion *stand* in the royal presence, both to betoken their reverence for their monarch, and their readiness to depart on the instant in the performance of the royal behests. They evidently pay earnest attention to the commands of the king.

The subject of this interview is no doubt Harold's intended expedition to the court of William. Unhappily, there is no point in history respecting which a greater diversity of statement exists among contemporary writers, than the visit of Harold to the court of William. Three views are taken of it :—one is, that Harold was commissioned by Edward to inform the young Duke of Normandy that he had been nominated by him as his successor to the throne ; another is, that Harold, whilst taking recreation in a fishing-boat, was accidentally carried out to sea, and driven on the shores of Ponthieu ; the third is, that Harold had begged permission of Edward to go into Normandy, in order to release from captivity two relatives, a brother and a nephew, who, after Earl Godwin's rebellion, had been placed as hostages in the hands of the Norman duke. The question for us to consider is which is the view countenanced by the Tapestry. Unfortunately, the inscription over the group is simply EDWARD REX, and, so, gives us no definite information. It will be well to examine the statements of the chroniclers, and then compare them with the representations of our worsted work.

William of Malmesbury says, "King Edward declining into years, as he had no children himself, and saw the sons of Godwin growing in power, despatched messengers to the King of Hungary to send over Edward, the son of his brother Edmund, with all his family; intending, as he declared, that either he, or his sons, should succeed to the hereditary kingdom of England, and that his own want of issue should be supplied by that of his kindred. Edward came in consequence, but died almost immediately. He left three surviving children; that is to say, Edgar, who, after the death of Harold, was by some elected king; and who, after many revolutions of fortune, is now living wholly retired in the country, in extreme old age;[a] Christina, who grew old at Romsey in the habit of a nun; and Margaret, whom Malcolm King of the Scots, espoused......The king, in consequence of the death of his relation, losing his first hope of support, gave the succession of England to William Earl of Normandy. He was well worthy of such a gift, being a young man of superior mind, who had raised himself to the highest eminence by his unwearied exertion; moreover, he was his nearest relation by consanguinity, as he was the son of Robert, the son of Richard the Second (of Normandy), whom we have repeatedly mentioned as the brother of Emma, Edward's mother. Some affirm that Harold himself was sent into Normandy by the King for this purpose; others, who knew Harold's more secret intentions, say, that being driven thither against his will by the violence of the wind, he imagined this device, in order to extricate

[a] *See* Note C., at the end of the Volume.

E

himself. This, as it appears nearest the truth, I shall relate. Harold being at his country seat at Bosham, went for recreation on board a fishing boat, and, for the purpose of prolonging his sport, put out to sea; when a sudden tempest arising, he was driven with his companions on the coast of Ponthieu. The people of that district, as was their native custom, immediately assembled from all quarters; and Harold's company, unarmed and few in number, were, as it might easily be, quickly overpowered by an armed multitude, and bound hand and foot. Harold, craftily meditating a remedy for this mischance, sent a person, whom he had allured by great promises, to William to say, that he had been sent into Normandy by the King, for the purpose of expressly confirming in person the message which had been imperfectly delivered by people of less authority, but that he was detained in fetters by Guy, and could not execute his embassy....By these means Harold was liberated at William's command, and conducted by Guy in person."[a]

Master Wace inclines to the opinion, that he went to rescue the hostages. His statement is, "When his father (Earl Godwin) had died, Harold, pitying the hostages, was desirous to cross over into Normandy, and bring them home. So he went to take leave of the King. But Edward strictly forbade him, and charged and conjured him not to go to Normandy, nor to speak with Duke William; for he might soon be drawn into some snare, as the Duke was very shrewd; and he told him that if he wished to have the hostages home, he would choose some messenger for the purpose.

[a] Bohn's edition, p. 253.

So at least I have found the story written. But another book tells me, that the King ordered him to go for the purpose of assuring Duke William, his cousin, that he should have the realm after his death. How the matter really was I never knew."[a]

Let us now attend to the questions, How are we to reconcile these various statements, and what is the view taken by the draftsman of the Tapestry?

We must at once abandon the fishing boat story. The preparation which Harold makes for his expedition, and the numbers he takes with him, are irreconcileable with this view. Besides, the ships do not seem to be suffering from stress of weather, and, according to the inscription, Harold appears to have made a prosperous voyage, ET VELIS VENTO PLENIS, VENIT IN TERRAM WIDONIS COMITIS—And his sails being filled with the wind, he came into the territory of Count Guy.

We must also abandon the view which represents him as going to procure, *in a direct and open manner*, the hostages which William held. He knew that William was as shrewd as he was ambitious, and would not be so simple as to give up at his request, however reasonable it might be, the only means he had of holding him in restraint. Besides, the Tapestry represents the King, in the first compartment, in the attitude of one giving a command, rather than administering advice. The interview which Harold has with the King, on his return, strengthens this view. *(Plate XII.)* Harold comes into the presence of the Confessor like a

[a] Taylor's Wace, p. 76.

guilty person, deploring his misdeeds and craving pardon. An axe, carried by an attendant on the left of the King, is turned towards him, apparently betokening that he has committed an offence worthy of death. The King is evidently reproving him sharply, but the attendant on the right of the King having the edge of his axe turned away from Harold, shows that the result of the interview was a pardon. The monarch was in fact too powerless to adopt any rigorous steps towards so influential a subject as the son of Godwin. If Harold had simply failed upon a private errand of his own, but which the King had forewarned him would be a bootless one, the King would have been more disposed to laugh at the trouble into which he had brought himself than take such serious notice of his conduct.

Besides, it is admitted on all hands, that Edward intended to appoint William as his successor, and most of the chroniclers agree in asserting that the Norman had already received some intimation of it. Further, William, after procuring the kingdom, always claimed to hold it, amongst other pleas, *Beneficio concessionis domini et cognati mei, gloriosi Regis Edwardi*—By the devise of my lord and relative the glorious King Edward.[a] Now, is it likely that a document which depicted the views of the Norman court would neglect to insert so important a title?

Supposing it to be a point established, that in the first compartment the Confessor is giving orders to Harold to inform William of the honours that awaited him, and abandoning, for the reasons

[a] General Introduction to Domesday, vol. i., p. 312.

already stated, the view of his being accidentally cast ashore on the coast of Ponthieu, we are necessarily led to suppose that he designedly shaped his course to that place, in order to promote his own ends. The Earl of Ponthieu was jealous of William's growing power, and had often been in arms against him. He had on one occasion been imprisoned by him for two years. Harold might readily suppose, that if he could obtain the assistance of Guy, he might, by stealth or stratagem, get possession of the persons of his brother and nephew. Hence, instead of going direct to Rouen, he seems to have shaped his course more to the north. He might argue with himself, that when once he had got possession of the hostages, the wrath of William, which would no doubt be aroused by the proceeding, would be easily allayed by his putting him in formal possession of the fact of his being appointed by the present occupant of the English crown his successor.

On the first view of the case, it seems strange that Harold should undertake an errand which was apparently so much opposed to his interests, or even that the King should intrust him with such a commission. Harold, however, could have little objection to make it known that it was the King's wish that William should be appointed his successor; for it was of some importance to him, having an eye to the crown himself, that the direct heir should, at all events, be superseded. Edgar Atheling, the next in the succession, was a rival in the palace itself; William the Norman was separated from him and the land of their mutual ambition by a barrier which was in those days a very formidable one—the English Channel.

If Harold entertained these views, he would take care to inform the King of his acquiescence in his well known intentions respecting the succession, and thus encourage him to send him upon his present errand.

This method of reconciling the different views given by the chroniclers upon this involved point of English history is, it must be confessed, purely theoretical; at the same time, no better occurs.

Harold has received his commission from the King; let us see how he fulfils it. He is first seen riding in company with several persons of distinction (as their dress indicates) to the place of embarkation. The legend here is, [U]BI HAROLD DUX ANGLORUM ET SUI MILITES EQUITANT AD BOSHAM—Where Harold the English chief and his knights ride to Bosham. Harold is represented twice in this group (by no means an unusual thing, as we shall afterwards see); once, lifting up his hand, as if in the attitude of command; and again, with his hawk upon his fist, to betoken his high rank; a pack of hounds are scampering before him.

The hawk and the hounds require a few words of remark. It is well known to persons conversant in antiquity, that the great men of those times had only two ways of being accoutred when they set out upon a journey; either in the habiliments of war, or for the chase. Harold, as going on an errand of peace, we find here represented in the latter. The bird upon the fist was a mark of high nobility. We see it frequently upon seals and miniatures, of that age, of ladies as well as men; and so sacred was this bird esteemed, that we find it prohibited in the ancient laws for any one to give his hawk or his sword as part of his ransom. Severe fines were laid on those who should steal another's hawk. Harold, it will be observed, is the only one of all his suite who has the bird upon his fist.[a]

Several hawks are introduced in the course of the Tapestry, but in no one case is the bird provided with a hood. The hood was introduced from the East about the year 1200, and as after its introduction it was considered an essential part of the equipment of the bird, its absence in the Tapestry is conclusive evidence of its comparatively early date.[b]

The three larger dogs have collars, provided with rings through which, most probably, the leash passed; the other two are of a smaller breed. The horses are hog-maned. Harold's horse, in the more forward instance, has some ornament entwined with its mane.

Bosham is a hamlet in Sussex, near to Chichester, which still retains its ancient name. It was a sea-port of some consequence in Saxon times, and we frequently read of its being the point of departure for persons going to the Continent. Bosham was the property of Harold, having been obtained by his father, Earl Godwin, from the Archbishop of Canterbury.

Among the endowed churches of England, that of Bosham was

[a] Ducarel's Antiquities of Normandy, Appendix, p. 4.

[b] The first account of the hood is in a book written in Latin by the Emperor Frederic II. *See* History of Inventions and Discoveries by John Beckmann, translated by William Johnston, vol. i. p. 330.

probably one of the richest. In the reign of King Edward it had land belonging to it to the extent of a hundred and twelve hides. The generality of church endowments were infinitely smaller. Hence we find the church represented in the Tapestry as a structure of considerable consequence.[a]

A tree closes the scene. It is of a species which does not flourish in our modern woods, but which nevertheless grows very abundantly in the MSS. of the tenth and eleventh centuries. Several of similar character may be seen in the Illustrations to Cædmon's *Metrical Paraphrase*, executed in the tenth century.[b] These trees, like the lions and leopards of the heralds of a subsequent date, were mere conventional forms, and not intended to be correct representations of the objects indicated.

The next compartment exhibits to us Harold and a companion (one no doubt being used to represent all) entering the sacred structure, with the view of seeking the divine blessing upon their enterprise. As the humility of their posture, when inside, could not be represented, the artist has exhibited them as entering it in a state of semi-genuflexion. In this he follows a classical model. Among the Greeks and Romans the act of adoration was expressed by the artists representing the body inclined slightly forwards, the knees gently bent, and the right hand touching the object of reverence.[c] Over the building which Harold and his companion enter is written the word ECCLESIA.—the church

---

[a] Introduction to Domesday, vol. i, p. 295.   [b] *See* Archæologia, vol. xxiv.
[c] Rich's Companion to the Latin Dictionary, art. *Adoratio.*

It is not a little curious to observe, that in immediate contiguity with the church in which our voyagers offer their devotions, is the festal board at which they comfort their own bowels, and pledge each other in goblets large as their own hearts. The scene is one of a truly Saxon character. Our blue-eyed forefathers never did things by halves, and whenever they sat down at the social table— and they did so as often as convenient—they exhibited a refreshing earnestness.

The scene represents the end of the feast, and hence the drinking horns rather than the platters are brought into requisition. Two of these are magnificent specimens, and remind us of the horn of Ulphe preserved in York Minster, and the Pusey horn. The individuals in the building are evidently pledging each other, and the challenged and the challenger are drinking in turn out of the same cup. Robert de Brunne refers to this practice in the following lines :—

> "This is their custom and their gest
> When thei are at the ale or fest;
> Ilk man that loves, where him think
> Sall say wassail, and to him drink.
> He that bids, sall say wassail;
> The tother sall say again drinkhail.
> That said wassail drinkes of the cup,
> Kissand his felow he gives it up;
> Drinkhail, he says, and drinkes thereof,
> Kissand him in bord and skoff."[a]

Besides horns, semicircular vessels, or mazer cups, appear among the furnishings of the board. These vessels were generally of

[a] Quoted in Taylor's Wace, p. 156.

F

wood, but occasionally of gold or silver. Our ancestors, who somewhat strangely blended religion with their festivities, not unfrequently had mottos, such as the following, inscribed upon their mazer bowls :—

𝔦𝔫 𝔱𝔥𝔢 𝔫𝔞𝔪𝔢 𝔬𝔣 𝔱𝔥𝔢 𝔱𝔯𝔦𝔫𝔦𝔱𝔦𝔢
𝔣𝔦𝔩𝔩𝔢 𝔱𝔥𝔢 𝔨𝔲𝔭 𝔞𝔫𝔡 𝔡𝔯𝔦𝔫𝔨 𝔱𝔬 𝔪𝔢.

But the best of friends must part. A messenger, who has blown the horn, to inform our voyagers that the boats are ready, till he is tired, comes personally, horn in hand, to urge their departure.

The scene of the embarkation is curious. Harold, the most powerful subject in England—if he can be called a subject—strips off his lower garments, and wades into the sea. His companions follow him in similar guise. Harold has, as usual, his hawk upon his fist, and he and his companion (the representative of the rest), more careful of their hounds than themselves, carry them dry-shod on board the ship that waits to receive them.

No satisfactory explanation has been given of the peculiar implement held in the left hand of the attendant who is next but one to Harold. Can it be a 'throw stick' such as was generally used by the ancient Egyptian sportsmen in fowling ?[b]

Harold has two ships, and they are represented twice over— once at their departure from the English coast, and again on their arrival at the shores of France. But before attending to the adven-

[b] *See* Sir J. Gardner Wilkinson's Popular Account of the Ancient Egyptians, vol. i, p. 235 ; and Bonomi's Nineveh, p. 136.

tures which befell the Saxon Earl on the opposite side, it will be well to review the ground already trodden, in order to gather up some fragments of information respecting the tastes and habits of the ancient English.

The architectural delineations of the Tapestry are those of the Conquest. Throughout the whole, the circular arch, which is characteristic of the Saxon and Norman styles, prevails in its simplest forms. Interlacing arches which occur so frequently in the later Norman buildings, and which are supposed to have introduced the pointed or Gothic style, never occur. The palace of Edward the Confessor, in the first compartment, is a large building as compared with the church and manor-house of Bosham in the second. In some of its details it bears a striking resemblance to the 'heavenly abode' in one of the early illustrations of Cædmon's Paraphrase.[a] Of the chequered work on the face of the chief buttress tower many examples exist to this day in Normandy. The chief feature of the church is the doorway, as is the case with all Norman buildings up to a late period. The windows are small and insignificant, and were probably unglazed. It is roofed with stone shingles or tiles, rounded at the lower extremity, and fastened to the framework with nails, as is conventionally represented in the drawing. The roofs in the Saxon illustrations already referred to present a precisely similar appearance. The traveller in Normandy will often be reminded by existing buildings of these arrangements. The house in which the voyagers take their

[a] Archæologia, vol. 24, plate LV.

farewell repast is worthy of observation. It is constructed upon the plan of the ancient "peel houses" of the North of England. The upper apartment has an independent entrance by stone steps from the outside, and seems to be the place of greatest comfort and security. The lower room is vaulted, and is divided into three compartments, like the aisles of a church. This was not an unusual arrangement in buildings of the Saxon and Norman period.[a]

The dress of the parties may be briefly described. It has manifestly been derived from a Roman model. A garment, doubtless of woollen, invests the body, and comes up to the neck. A tunic, having something of the form of a frock coat, is put on over this, and is bound round the waist by a girdle. In the horsemen, this tunic is brought below the knees, and, for greater convenience in riding, is divided so as to form two wide loose legs. Most of the men are furnished with hose, which fit tightly, and come well up the thigh. Most of them also are furnished with shoes, which seem to fit the foot naturally and easily. In addition to these coverings, the superior orders wear a cloak, nearly resembling the *chlamys* of the Roman general, and which is fastened by a fibula, or brooch, at the right shoulder.

All the figures, excepting those accoutred with crowns or helmets, are bare-headed. This at first sight does not seem to be the case; the heads of the parties appear as if they were enveloped with caps of various colours. It will be observed, however, that, within

[a] Illustrations of Cædmon's Paraphrase. Archæologia, vol. xxiv., p. 339, plate LXXV. Hudson Turner's Domestic Architecture of England, vol. i., p. 4.

doors as well as without, their heads wear the same appearance. But the shaven crown of the priests reveals the fact. These personages appear with hair as indisputably red, and blue, and yellow, as the rest, yet they show the bare poll in the centre. *(See Plates VI. and XIII.)* It may also be observed that the hinder part of the heads of the Frenchmen is bare. In France, at this period, an absurd custom prevailed of shaving the back of the head. The men of Normandy and Ponthieu accordingly appear as if they had caps stuck upon the front of their heads, leaving the back part naked. All this seems to prove that, at the time of the Conquest, it was not customary either in England or France for men to cover the head, except for defensive purposes in the day of battle.

The Saxons are uniformly represented with mustaches; the French are not. King Edward always appears with a beard. The Saxons were fond of cultivating the hair, and exhibiting full and flowing locks. In the youthful days of King Edward both razors and scissors were eschewed. In process of time, however, through some silvery influence, men were induced to denude their chins of nature's covering. Frenchmen made a clean sweep of it, but the Saxons held out for the mustache. King Edward maintained the customs of his youth, and he is always represented on coins, medals, and the Tapestry, with all the capillary attractions which nature ever gave him. In these respects, the Tapestry is true to history.

In ancient times, as well as in modern, fashions were subject to change. In the reigns immediately succeeding the Conqueror's, modes prevailed different from those depicted in the Tapestry. The points of the shoes were elongated, greater extravagance of dress was indulged in, and the Normans, instead of shaving their hair like monks, suffered it to grow ridiculously long; beards, too, were cultivated. The following summary of the fashions of the late Norman period is to our present purpose :—

" During the reigns of Rufus and Henry I. the dress of the higher classes became much more costly in material and extravagant in shape. Some most ridiculous fashions are reprobated and caricatured by the historians and illuminators of that period. The sleeves of the tunics were made long enough to cover and hang considerably below the hand. Peaked-toed boots and shoes of the most absurd shapes, some terminating like a scorpion's tail, others stuffed with tow and curling round like a ram's horn, are mentioned by the monkish historians. Ordericus Vitalis says they were invented by some one deformed in the foot. The mantles and tunics were worn much longer and fuller, and the former lined with the most expensive furs. Henry I. is said to have had one presented to him by the Bishop of Lincoln, lined with black sable with white spots, and which cost £100. of the money of that day.

" The English now, both Saxon and Norman, suffered their hair to grow to an immoderate length instead of being cropped ridiculously short; and William of Malmesbury, who has previously complained of his countrymen having imitated the latter fashion, now laments over the long hair, the loose flowing garments, the pointed shoes, and effeminate appearance of the English generally.

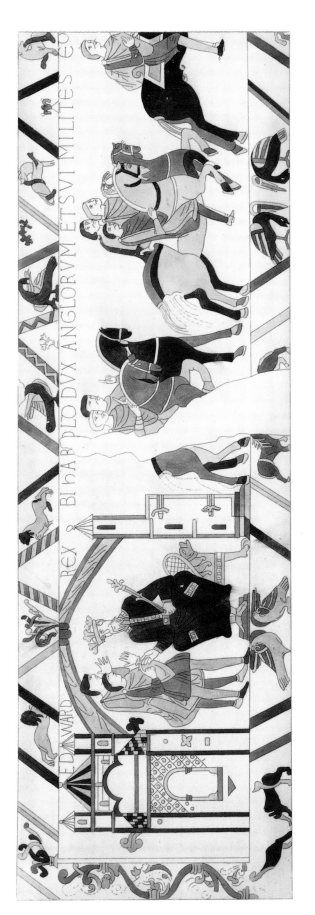

I. HAROLD ATTENDS THE COURT OF KING EDWARD BEFORE HIS JOURNEY TO NORMANDY.

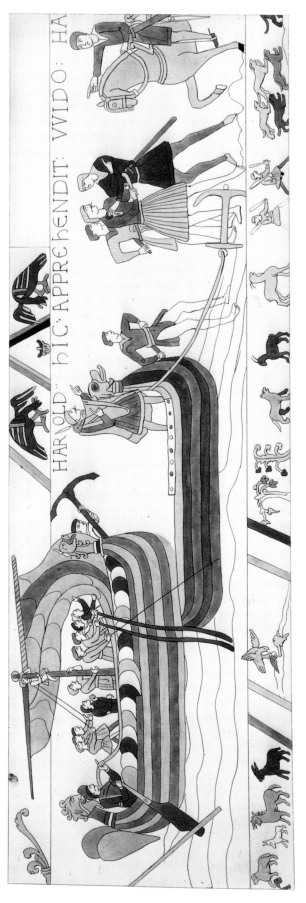

II. HAROLD CROSSES THE ENGLISH CHANNEL AND IS MADE PRISONER BY GUY, COUNT OF PONTHIEU.

III. TAKEN IN CAPTIVITY TO THE CASTLE OF BEAURAIN, HAROLD MEETS GUY.

IV. DUKE WILLIAM OF NORMANDY HEARS OF HAROLD'S CAPTURE.

V. HAROLD IS TAKEN TO ROUEN, WHERE HE IS RECEIVED BY THE DUKE.

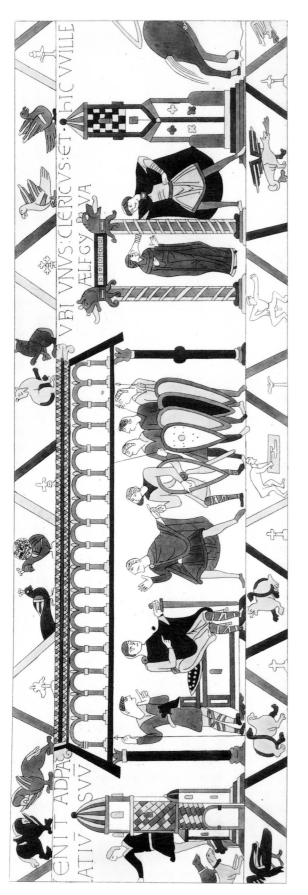

VI. HAROLD ACCOMPANIES WILLIAM'S EXPEDITION AGAINST CONAN, EARL OF BRETAGNE.

VII. THE NORMAN ARMY PASSES MOUNT ST. MICHAEL.

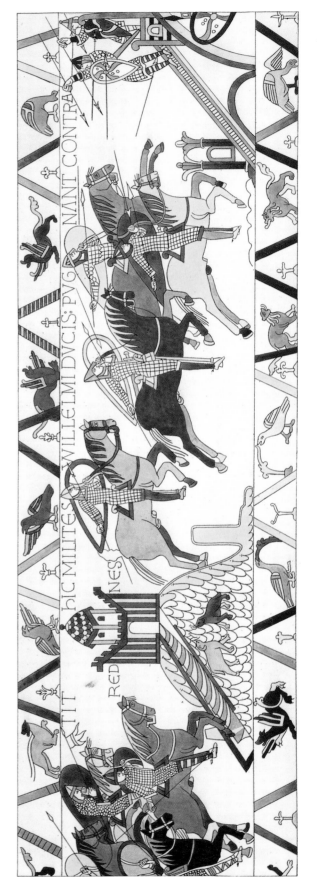

VIII. HAROLD RESCUES TWO MEN FROM QUICKSANDS; THE BRITTANY CAMPAIGN PROCEEDS.

Even long beards were worn during the reign of Henry I.; and Ordericus Vitalis compares the men of that day to 'filthy goats.'

"Anselm, Archbishop of Canterbury, refused his benediction on Ash Wednesday to those who would not cut their hair. Councils were held on this important matter. The razor and the scissors were not only recommended *ex cathedra*, but positively produced sometimes at the end of a sermon against the sinfulness of long locks and curling mustaches. Serlo d'Abon, Bishop of Seez, on Easter Day, 1105, after preaching against beards before Henry I., cropped not only that of the king but those of the whole congregation with a pair of scissors he had provided for the occasion. But nothing could long repress these fashions, which in the time of Stephen again raged to such an extent that the fops of the day suffered their hair to grow till they looked more like women than men; and those whose ringlets were not sufficiently luxurious added false hair to equal or surpass in appearance their more favoured brethren." [a]

We can only account for the exact conformity of the manners and customs depicted in the Tapestry with those prevailing during the Conqueror's reign, on the supposition that the Tapestry was then produced.

[a] Pictorial History of England, vol. i. p. 637.

III. THE ENTANGLEMENT.

"Sir, what ill chance hath brought you to this place?"
Paradise Regained.

WHEN Robert of Normandy went on pilgrimage to Jerusalem, he named his son William, then a boy seven years of age, his heir. His courtiers expressing their fears that during his absence the estates would be left without a head, he replied, "Not so, by my faith, not so! I will leave you a master in my place. I have a little bastard here; he is little, indeed, but he will grow; nay, by God's grace, I have great hopes that he will prove a gallant man; therefore I do pray you all to receive him from my hands, for from this time forth I give him seisin of the duchy of Normandy, as my known and acknowledged heir." William, who was destined never again to see his father, was committed to the guardianship of his two uncles—"a lamb to the tutelage of wolves." When, at a very early age, he was compelled to take the reins of government into his own hands, he had a difficult part to perform. As the author of the *Roman de Rou* informs us, "The feuds against him were many, and his friends few; for he found that most were ill inclined towards him; those even whom his father held dear he found haughty and evil disposed. The barons warred upon each other;

the strong oppressed the weak, and he could not prevent it."[a] The success which attended his efforts made him an object of jealousy and fear. In 1054 the King of France made war upon him, with the intention of depriving him of his duchy. In the battle of Mortemer, William overcame the forces of France, and, along with some others, took Guy Count of Ponthieu prisoner.

Harold knew well the difficult part which his rival had to perform, and doubtless thought to take advantage of it. If he could induce Guy to interest himself in the fate of his brother and nephew, who were detained as hostages at the court of Normandy, the assistance of the King of France and of many of his great barons could easily be secured. Such, probably, was the reasoning of Harold, as he stepped on board his ship at Bosham. The territories of Guy lay immediately to the north of those of William. Let us see how the voyager fares. No untoward accident occurs on the passage across, but all is expectation and anxiety as the ships approach the shore. One man from the top of the mast of the hindermost vessel eagerly spies out the land, the whole of the crew are standing up and looking anxiously toward it. They evidently discern indications which make them doubtful of a hospitable reception. This ship, however, bears no marks of having encountered a gale. Its sail is fully extended, and is in good order.

The foremost vessel contains Harold alone, as the superscription, HAROLD, informs us. He is in full dress, ready to pay his respects

[a] Taylor's Wace, page 7.

G

to the Count of Ponthieu. He is, however, armed with a spear, which evidently indicates that he has reason to fear that he is in an enemy's country.

The next group of figures reveals the plot. Guy, accompanied by a troop of horsemen bearing sword and shield and spear, orders the arrest of Harold and his companions. The Count is simply clad, but well armed; he has not only a sword of portentous size attached to his side, but a basilard, or hunting knife, suspended from his saddle. " As an instance of that peculiar accuracy which is observed by the designer of the Tapestry, even in seemingly unimportant particulars, and which makes the work so much more interesting as a faithful depiction of the various circumstances of the times, we find the Norman horses of this and other groups are represented as being larger than the Anglo-Saxon. The hair of the mane is also uncut, and falls on the neck; the saddle and its accoutrements are similar."[a] Harold, stripped, as before, for disembarkation, is immediately seized. The first impression on the minds of the party evidently is to resist. Their ordinary weapons, which have for the moment been laid aside, are not at hand; but that weapon which a Saxon never laid aside—that weapon, half knife, half dagger, with which he divided his food at meals, which he had by him even during the hours of sleep, and which was deposited in his grave when his warfare was o'er—that weapon, the

[a] This observation, together with some others which may not in every case require to be specially noted, has been taken from a clever series of papers on the Bayeux Tapestry, which were published in the *Ladies' Newspaper* for 1851-2.

saxe, from which, according to the mediæval rhymer Gotfridus Viterbiensis, the Saxons derived their name —

> "Ipse brevis gladius apud illos Saxo vocatur,
> Unde sibi Saxo nomen peperisse notatur." [a]

— is clutched and drawn.

The latter figures of the group, by the hesitancy of their manner, seem to say that resistance is useless; each has instinctively laid hold of his weapon, but it rests midway in his girdle.

The inscription over this group is, HIC APPREHENDIT WIDO HAROLDUM ET DUXIT EUM AD BELREM ET IBI EUM TENUIT.—Here Guy seized Harold, and led him to Beaurain, where he detained him prisoner. The modern Beaurain is situated a short distance from Montreuil, the capital of the ancient province of Ponthieu. A tree closes the scene.

In the solitude of his prison Harold must have reflected bitterly upon his rashness in committing himself to the hands of Guy without having accurately ascertained his feelings towards him. Instead of a friend he found in him a foe. Instead of furthering his views he involved him in almost inextricable difficulties. The Count, probably, had too keen a sense of William's power again to run the risk of incurring his wrath; he therefore resolved, to avoid all appearance of ambiguity, to detain Harold as a prisoner, and to extract from his friends as large a sum as possible in the shape of ransom. It gives us a curious insight into the state of society in those days, to observe that no

[a] Akerman on Celtic and Teutonic Weapons.—*Archæ.*, vol. xxxiv.

one disputed the right of Guy to seize the person and property of a stranger, who, without hostile intent, had ventured upon his shores, or, as some believe, had been driven there by mischance. Harold had no friend at hand to release him from his unpleasant position. His active and clever rival, William of Normandy, hearing of his circumstances, immediately put forth the most strenuous and apparently generous efforts to effect his enlargement, thereby laying him under very serious obligations. It is the object of the succeeding portions of the Tapestry to place these efforts in a strong light, and by implication to show the ingratitude of Harold in opposing William's claims to the English throne.

The first scene represents Harold proceeding to the residence of his captor. The expression given to the unlucky Earl is one of deep dejection. He is stripped of the cloak which marked his nobility; and though he carries his hawk upon his fist, its usual posture is reversed, an intimation that his hawking days are over. Harold is well guarded by a party of armed horsemen. Guy rides before, clad in the decorative mantle of his rank, and having the falcon upon his fist, with its head advanced as if ready to take wing. The artist has very successfully portrayed in the countenance of Guy the chuckling conceit of this heartless chieftain in the possession of so rich a prize as Harold.

The next group of standing figures is supposed to represent some of Harold's party, distinguished by the mustache, in custody of Guy's soldiers.

Harold, indignant at the unjust treatment which he had received, sought an interview with the Count, no doubt feeling sure that he would be able to make such a representation of his case, or to offer such inducements, as would infallibly lead to his immediate release. An interview was granted. The inscription over the next scene is "UBI HAROLD ET WIDO PARABOLANT"—Where Harold and Guy converse. Guy is seated *(Plate III.)* with great pomp upon an elevated seat. His throne is less ornate than that of the Confessor, to mark no doubt the difference between a King and a Count, and it is without a cushion, but it is decorated with dogs' heads and claws, which are so frequently introduced into all the work of that period. His feet, as is usual with persons of rank, rest upon a footstool, having in this instance three steps. Guy holds a naked sword with its point turned upwards; he is attended by a guard, who is armed with a sword of prodigious size, and a spear. This attendant touches the elbow of his chief with one hand, and with the forefinger of the other points to some object, probably the messengers of William, who are now approaching. Harold, though suffered to wear the chlamys of nobility, comes into the presence of the haughty Count in a slightly inclining posture. He feels he is at the mercy of his captor. He has a sword, but its point is directed to the ground. His companion has neither cloak nor sword. From the arrogant bearing of Guy in this picture we cannot doubt that the unhappy Harold returned to his prison more disconsolate than before.

But, help was at hand. There is a figure, which we have not observed, at one extremity of the audience chamber. He is a very attentive but apparently an unobserved witness of the interview. His party-coloured dress and the vandyked fringe of his tunic have suggested the idea that this personage is the court jester.[a] The court fool was usually a very shrewd person, and having, on account of his presumed simplicity, access to his master at all times, was a very convenient agent in court intrigue. This wily personage seems to have found means to acquaint William with the untoward position of the English ambassador, for the next scene is entitled UBI NUNTII WILIELMI DUCIS VENERUNT AD WIDONEM—Where the messengers of William came to Guy.

William on one occasion owed his life to the friendly interference of a jester. Wace thus relates the story:—Guy of Burgundy, who was a near relative of William's, became envious of him, and resolved to disinherit him. Assembling several powerful barons, who were as discontented as himself, he said, " There was not any heir who had a better right to Normandy than himself....He was no bastard, but born in wedlock ; and if right was done, Normandy would belong to him. If they would support him in his claim, he would divide it with them." So, at length, he said so much, and promised so largely, that they swore to support him according to their power in making war on William,and to seek his disherison by force or treason. Then they stored their castles, dug fosses, and erected barricades, William knowing nothing of their preparations. He was at that time sojourning at Valognes, for his pleasure as well as on business ; and had been engaged for several days hunting and

[a] Mr. Charles Stothard in the Archæologia, vol. xix, p. 189.

shooting in the woods. One evening, late, his train had left his court, and all had gone to rest at the hostels where they lodged, except those who were of his household; and he himself was laid down. Whether he slept or not, I do not know, but in the season of the first sleep, a fool named Golet came, with a staff slung at his neck, crying out at the chamber door, and beating the wall with the staff; "*Ovrez!*" said he, "*ovrez! ovrez!* ye are dead men: *levez! levez!* Where art thou laid, William? Wherefore dost thou sleep? If thou art found here thou wilt die; thy enemies are arming around; if they find thee here thou wilt never quit the Cotentin, nor live till the morning!" Then William was greatly alarmed; he rose up, and stood as a man sorely dismayed. He asked no further news, for it seemed unlikely to bring him any good. He was in his breeches and shirt, and putting a cloak around his neck, he seized his horse quickly, and was soon upon the road. I know not whether he even stopped to seek for his spurs, but he hasted on till he came to the fords nearest at hand, which were those of Vire, and crossed them by night in fear and great anger.[a]

Had the fool not thus opportunely aroused him—had he not acted with peculiar promptitude—had he not received important assistance in the course of his journey from a faithful vassal, who facilitated his flight, and led his pursuers off the track—we should never have heard of William the Conqueror. As it was, he got safely next day to his own castle at Falaise. "If he were in bad plight," says Wace, "what matters it, so that he got safe."

[a] Taylor's Wace, p. 11.

The result of the fool's interference in behalf of Harold soon appears. We are now introduced to two personages, sent by Duke William, who, in their master's name, demand the deliverance of the captive. Guy is standing, and wears a haughty air. He holds an axe in his hand, by way of asserting that he has the power of life or death over his prisoner. He is partially habited in the costume of war. Under his chlamys he wears a tunic of scale armour, probably composed of overlapping pieces of leather. This dress, though not so secure as one of mail, would nevertheless present considerable resistance to the stroke of a weapon. Odo is represented as wearing a dress somewhat similar in the battle of Hastings; also a figure which I take to be William approaching Mount St. Michael. His hose are composed of party-coloured materials; several other personages in the Tapestry, chiefly individuals of consequence, are so adorned. The Saxons, and probably the Normans also, were in the habit of protecting their legs in the day of battle by binding them round with slips of leather or other material. Guy has an armed attendant, standing aloof, but ready to act; and the two messengers of William apparently press their mission with great vigour. The legend of this is, UBI NUNTII WILIELMI DUCIS VENERUNT AD WIDONEM—Where the messengers of Duke William came to Guy. The horses of the messengers stand hard by, held by a *dwarf*, who, although he wears a beard, is evidently a Norman, for his hair is shaven off the back of his head. Over this little fellow, in the Tapestry, is written the word TUROLD. Who this personage was we have no means of knowing.

He may have been some favourite with the ladies employed upon the embroidery, who adopted this mode of conferring immortality upon him; or, as Miss Agnes Strickland has suggested, he may have been the artist who was employed to design the Tapestry, and who, though he could not with historic truth be introduced into any of the principal scenes, yet, very laudably, wished for a place upon the canvas. It is, however, important to observe, that the son of a person named Turold occurs in the Domesday Survey, among the under-tenants of Odo, Bishop of Bayeux, for the county of Essex.[a] The celebrated Norman ballad *The Song of Roland* seems to have had for its author a person of the name of Turold, if we may credit its concluding lines, "And so endeth the history sung of Turoldus."[b] This inscription bears upon the subject of the authenticity of the Tapestry. Had the work been constructed some considerable period after the events which it describes, it must have been compiled from historic documents, and so have contained none but historic personages. As it is, there are several individuals introduced to us in the Tapestry of which we have no trace in the chronicles of the day, but with which the draftsman takes it for granted that all are as familiar as himself—a very natural and very common oversight. The house, divided into three aisles after the manner of that in which Harold took his parting feast, is probably intended to represent the palace of the Count.

These messengers having reported their ill success to Duke William, he immediately sends two others, who gallop to Beaurain

[a] Introduction to Domesday, vol. ii. p. 404. [b] The Song of Roland, London, 1854.

H

at the utmost speed of their horses. Over them is the inscription, NUNTII WILLELMI—The messengers of William. A watchman, elevated upon a tree, observes the movements of this second embassy, probably with the view of giving William the earliest intelligence respecting it. All this is cleverly designed, in order to show the deep interest which William took in the welfare of his captive friend, who was afterwards, according to the court version of the story, to repay him with so much ingratitude. These horsemen wear a threatening aspect; they are armed with spear, shield, and sword; their spears are pointed threateningly towards the place of their destination. Their shields bear a curious device, a winged dragon whose tail is twisted in a peculiar manner. This object is one of constant occurrence in the Tapestry, and seems to be one of superstitious reverence. Harold's standard is a dragon. The standard of the Dacians, as depicted in Trajan's Column, is a dragon. We have some others introduced into the ornamental border of the Tapestry. In the illustrations of *Cædmon's Paraphrase*, the great dragon Satan is in two instances figured in a guise nearly resembling these. Whilst in a heathen state the Saxons and Normans doubtless made the evil one an object of worship, as most heathen nations have done, and, long after their reception of Christianity, may, though with questionable taste, have retained for ornamental purposes the emblem which they had been accustomed to regard with superstitious reverence.

The transactions we are now considering probably occurred in the spring of the year at the close of which King Edward died. In the lower margin of the scenes just reviewed the operations of husbandry peculiar to that season are portrayed. One man is ploughing. The plough has wheels, and is very similar to some that are figured in *Cædmon's Paraphrase*. Next comes a sower casting the seed into the ground. He conducts the operation precisely as it has been conducted from that day to this. Next follows a harrow, drawn by an ox, which wears the yoke upon its neck. This method of yoking oxen is still common in Normandy.

We are not certain what means William used to bring Guy to his views. Some chroniclers say he coaxed him, some say he threatened him, and several maintain that he bribed him by giving him a large tract of land. This however is certain, that he succeeded in inducing him to relax his hold of Harold.

The next compartment of the Tapestry exhibits to us William seated on a throne near his castle gate. He is receiving a messenger, who approaches him on bended knees. The superscription is, HIC VENIT NUNTIUS AD WILGELMUM DUCEM—Here a messenger came to Duke William. The peculiarity of the spelling of the Duke's name WILGELMUS need not surprise us. At that day, and for long afterwards, the orthography even of proper names was not fixed. The G would no doubt be sounded like *y* or the diphthong *ie*, as is still the case in certain words in some parts of the North of England. Who the messenger is we are not informed; he is evidently a Saxon, and is probably one of Harold's companions, who has accompanied William's ambassadors to Rouen, by way of giving the Duke a pledge of the success of their commission.

Guy having agreed to deliver up his prisoner, resolves to make a merit of doing so, and conducts him in person to William's court. The Duke, desirous of doing all honour to his expected guest, goes out to meet him. When the two parties approach, Guy very officiously introduces Harold to the Duke, and seems to expect great commendations for his zeal and activity. Harold himself follows Guy, having once again the mantle of gentle birth on his left shoulder, and carrying his hawk upon his fist, looking forward, in token of liberty. William sits firmly upon his horse; his manner is quiet, but very decided; his figure is that of a strong, square-built man. We know that his muscular powers were very considerable; this is probably no fancy portrait.

The inscription over this compartment is, HIC WIDO ADDUXIT HAROLDUM AD WILGELMUM NORMANNORUM DUCEM—Here Guy led Harold to William Duke of the Normans.

William now accompanies his guest to his palace—probably at Rouen. A man from a gateway tower looks out and receives the party. The palace of William is a large and splendid structure. Both it and the castle we last noticed contrast strongly with those we have previously seen. The Normans were great builders. Whilst they were frugal in their household expenditure, they erected elegant habitations for themselves; the Saxons on the other hand (at least so say the chroniclers) did not care how they were lodged, but laid out large sums in eating and drinking.[a] William has a guard standing at his back. A Saxon is addressing him

---

[a] William of Malmesbury, (Bohn's edition) p. 279.

with considerable vehemence upon some business relating to the French soldiers, to whom he points. The speaker is probably Harold; but what the subject of conference is, can only be a subject of conjecture. Can it be that he is requesting the assistance of an escort to accompany a messenger of his to England to inform his friends of his happy release from captivity?

In the border above the palace are a pair of pea-fowls. This is probably intended to give us an idea of the splendour of William's court. In the middle ages no feast was complete excepting this bird made its appearance on the table, arrayed, after being taken from the spit, in all its gorgeous plumage. The feathers of this bird were in great request among our Saxon nobles as a means of decorating their halls.

The next compartment presents great difficulties. It is headed, UBI UNUS CLERICUS ET ÆLFGYVA—Where a clerk and Ælfgyva [converse]. It evidently refers to a transaction with which the court of Duke William were well acquainted, but of which the chroniclers have given us no account.

Ælfgyva is a Saxon word, signifying a present from the genii.[a] Emma, the wife of Ethelred, and some other English Queens, are occasionally by Saxon authors styled Ælfgyva; hence the term has been considered a descriptive title rather than a proper name. On this account some writers conceive that Queen Matilda is the individual here presented to our notice. If, however, the term Ælfgyva was a descriptive one, and applicable only to a Saxon Queen, it could

[a] Thierry's Norman Conquest (London, 1841), p. 41.

not at this period of the narrative belong to her, for William had not then obtained the English throne. Other authors consider that Agatha, a daughter of William, is the lady in question. Her name is written by Wace, Ele; and by some authors she is confounded with her sister Adeliza. When Harold swore to support William in his pretensions to the throne, he agreed to receive Agatha in marriage. This lady's subsequent history is confused. William of Malmesbury says she died before she was marriageable. Ordericus Vitalis gives the following account of her—"His daughter Agatha, who had been betrothed to Harold, was afterwards demanded in marriage by Alphonzo, King of Galicia, and delivered to his proxies to be conducted to him. But she, who had lost her former spouse, who was to her liking, felt extreme repugnance to marry another. The Englishman she had seen and loved, but the Spaniard she was more averse to because she had never set eyes on him. She therefore fervently prayed to God that she might never be carried into Spain, but that he would rather take her to himself. Her prayers were heard, and she died a virgin while she was upon the road." She, however, cannot be the Ælfgyva of the Tapestry. Making every allowance for the varities of her name, it would scarcely have been so written in her father's court; as she was never Queen, the descriptive epithet could not with propriety have been applied to her; and as at the time of Harold's visit to Normandy she was but a child, we cannot suppose that any formal embassage would be sent to her respecting the release of the English Earl, or any other subject.

The lady in question is probably Algitha, the widow of Griffith King of Wales, and sister to Edwin and Morcar, Earls of Mercia and Northumberland, whom Harold must have married shortly after his return to England, as his second wife.[a] Her name, as it is written by Florence of Worcester, and some other chroniclers, differs but little from Ælfgyva; besides, as Queen of England, she was entitled to the epithet. If this supposition be correct, the force of the introduction of this lady and the clerk into the Tapestry is considerable. The whole object of this part of the drawing is to display in glowing colours the generous kindness of William and the base treachery of Harold. Now if, as we may reasonably suppose, Harold had set his affections upon this lady before his departure for Normandy, and if, as we have conjectured, he had, on being rescued, sent, by William's assistance, messengers to England to announce his safety, a special and loving message to the queen of his affections would not be forgotten. The clerk certainly approaches her in a jocose manner, and undoubtedly has some agreeable intelligence to communicate. Now if Harold acted thus while enjoying William's hospitality, and solemnly un-

---

[a] The following passages from the *Chronicle of Florence of Worcester* furnish distinct evidence as to the marriage of Harold with Algitha:—" Regnavit autem Haraldus mensibus IX. et diebus totidem. Cujus morte audita, comites Eadwinus et Morcarus, qui se cum suis certamini subtraxere, Lundoniam venere, et sororem suam *Algitham reginam* sumptam ad civitatem Legionum misere." "Anno regni XXIII. rex Anglorum Eadwardus decessit. Cui ex ipsius concessione comes Haroldus, filius Godwini West-Saxonum ducis....successit; qui de *regina Aldgitha*, comitis Alfgari filia, habuit filium Haroldum; eodemque anno a Normanorum comite Willelmo peremptus est in bello."—*Monumenta Historica*, pp. 614, 642.

dertaking to marry his daughter Agatha as soon as she became of fitting age, his conduct was most unjustifiable; and it was peculiarly suitable to the object for which the Tapestry was prepared to expose it. Harold, before leaving England, may have placed his lady for temporary protection in some nunnery, which we may suppose to be indicated by the narrow and confined building in which Ælfgyva stands. In this case none was so proper to approach her as a priest. The employment of a person of the clerical order was moreover necessary, as few of the laity could read or write. The individual in the Tapestry has a shaven crown, but is dressed in ordinary attire. William of Malmesbury tells us that the Saxon clergy were not fond of any distinctive dress.

In the whole course of the Tapestry only three females are presented to our view—Ælfgyva, a mourning relative by the dying bed of the Confessor, and a woman forced by the flames from her dwelling at Hastings. This circumstance surely proves the modesty and retiring habits of the Saxon and Norman ladies.

As our ladies are scarce, let us pay them minute attention. The dress of the Saxon women varied very little during the long period that elapsed between the eighth and the end of the eleventh century; by thoroughly enveloping the whole body, it consulted the modest feelings of the sex, whilst its graceful folds gave considerable elegance to the person. Antiquaries are inquiring men. They do not like to leave any subject unexamined. That judicious inquirer, Strutt, finds some little difficulty in investigating the undermost garment worn by the Saxon ladies; he manages it, however, with great adroitness and delicacy. His words are worth quoting :—

"In the foregoing chapter it has been clearly proved that the shirt formed part of the dress of the men; and surely we cannot hesitate a moment to conclude that the women were equally tenacious of delicacy in their habit, and of course were not destitute of body-linen : the remains of antiquity it is true afford not sufficient authority to prove the fact; yet the presumptive argument founded upon female delicacy weighs so strongly in the scale, that I conclude this supposition to be consonant with the truth."[a] Over this undermost garment came another, which was only seen when the lower portion of the *gunna*, or gown, had been pushed aside; it was made of linen or some other light material. Next came the gown, consisting usually of some strong stuff. It fell down to the feet, and was sometimes girt round the waist by a band. The sleeves near the wrist were usually made very full, and hung down after the manner lately in use among ourselves. A mantle was worn over this by ladies of rank. It was probably fastened by a fibula, or brooch. The woman coming out of the burning house *(Plate XXII)* belongs probably to the lower orders, for she has not a mantle. A head-cover, or kerchief, was an indispensable part of the dress of Saxon ladies, whether high or low. It enveloped the head, concealing the hair entirely; the ends of it fell upon the shoulders.

In the time of Rufus and Henry I. the dress of the ladies, which had remained so long stationary, felt the stimulus of the Conquest.

[a] Planche's Strutt, vol. i., p. 14.

I

"The sleeves of their robes and their kerchiefs appear in the illuminations of that period knotted up, to prevent their trailing on the ground. Some of the sleeves have cuffs hanging from the wrist down to the heels, and of the most singular forms."[a] An ancient monk has drawn the evil one attired in this way, in order no doubt to throw discredit upon the fashion. The hair also was no longer concealed, but hung down in plaits on each side of the person as far as the waist. A statue of Matilda, wife of Henry I., on the west door-way of Rochester Cathedral, exhibits this usage. Had the Tapestry been executed in the days of this Queen, Ælfgyva's sleeves would have been fuller than they are, and her hair would have hung down in graceful ringlets.

[a] Pict. Eng., vol. i., p. 637.

IV. THE KNIGHTHOOD.

"Young knight whatever, that dost armes professe,
And through long labours huntest after fame,
Beware of fraud"——

Faerie Queene

WHEN Rollo and his brave companions, emigrating from Northern Europe at the end of the ninth century, got a firm hold of Rouen and the surrounding district, they were as far from being satisfied as ever. They ravaged every part of France, carrying their arms even into Burgundy. Charles the Simple, who had already yielded Normandy to them, harrassed by these unceasing hostilities, sought to purchase peace by the cession of another portion of his dominions. He offered Rollo the land between the river Epte and Brittany, if he would become a Christian and live in peace; but, though Charles threw his daughter into the scale, Rollo would not agree, for the territory was too small, and the lands uncultivated. He next offered him Flanders, which, by the way, was not his to give; but Rollo rejected it because it was boggy and full of marshes. He then offered him Brittany, which Rollo accepted.[a] Brittany, however, claimed to be a free state, and its inhabitants were a spirited and energetic race, not likely to yield allegiance where none was due.

[a] Thierry's History of the Normans, p. 36.

In accepting Brittany, therefore, Rollo obtained little better than an old quarrel. Continual wars, and a national enmity, between the states, was the only result of the gift.

We can here scarcely help observing by what a rare conjunction of circumstances it was that William, who from his boyhood had been at war with all the neighbouring states, and who a few months before the invasion of England, was engaged in active hostilities with the Count of Brittany, had leisure to undertake the great event of his life, could leave his duchy and drain it of his troops, without being exposed to the devastations of angry neighbours, and, not only so, but could obtain for his great enterprise the powerful assistance of those rival chiefs with whom he had so often been at variance, not even excepting the Counts of Ponthieu and Brittany. The most careless observer cannot but mark in this the finger of Providence.

But to return to our worsted work. Conan Earl of Bretagne being at this juncture at war with Duke William, and having drawn the Earl of Anjou into alliance with him, the two naturally agreed upon a given day to invade Normandy with their united forces. The Duke was however too much upon his guard, and too lively, to wait for them in his own dominions. He raised a considerable body of troops; and, knowing Harold to be a brave soldier, and fond of showing his valour, invited him and his companions to go with him upon this expedition; which Harold readily agreed to do. This was a clever stroke of policy. He not only procured the valuable assistance of Harold and his companions, all the more valuable in consequence of the experience they had gained in Wales, but obtained ample opportunities of studying the character of the man whom he could not but look upon as his great rival. He had the means, in their lengthened intercourse, of showing him great attentions, and thus of apparently laying him under great obligations. But, above all, he induced Harold by this step to excite the enmity of the men of Brittany against himself. That William should make war upon them was no more than the custom of the country, but what right had the Saxon to interfere in their affairs? They could not, and did not, forget this on the field of Hastings.

The campaign in Brittany is described more fully in the Tapestry than in any of the chronicles, and some events are there depicted, such as the surrender of Dinan, which are not mentioned in any of them. William and his party setting out upon their expedition *(Plate VII)* pass the neighbourhood of Mount St. Michael. The inscription is, HIC WILLEM DUX ET EXERCITUS EJUS VENERUNT AD MONTEM MICHAELIS—Here Duke William and his army came to Mount St. Michael. This mount consists of a solitary cone of granite rising out of a wide, level expanse of sand, which at high tide is nearly covered by the sea. It is a very conspicuous object, and is seen on all sides from a great distance. A little to the south of St. Michael's Mount, the river Coësnon, which forms the boundary between Normandy and Brittany, joins the sea. At this point the waters of the ocean, in consequence of the contracting boundaries of the bay lying between Brest and Cape la Hogue, rise with great impetuosity and to a great height. The fording of the river, therefore, in the vicinity of the sea is often a hazardous undertaking. To add to the difficulties of travellers, the sand which covers the plain around St. Michael's Mount, and extends some distance inland and along the bed of the river, is an exceedingly fine, white, marly dust, which, when covered with water, affords most treacherous footing. The beds of sand, moreover, frequently shift according to the varying currents of the tide, so that even a well accustomed traveller may get wrong. These statements have prepared us for the disasters which befel the party in crossing into Brittany. The legend here is, ET HIC TRANSIERUNT FLUMEN COSNONIS—And here they crossed the river Coësnon—Most of the group, mistrusting the treacherous ford, have dismounted. One individual more venturesome than the rest reaps the consequences of his rashness. All those on foot do not, however, entirely escape. Harold is represented rescuing two of them from their difficulties; one he bears upon his back, the other he drags by the hand. The inscription is—HIC HAROLD DUX TRAHEBAT EOS DE ARENA—Here Harold the Earl dragged them out of the quicksand.

The fishes and the eels in the lower border are an appropriate ornament. The draftsman has here indulged in a little play of fancy. A man, with knife in hand, in trying to catch one of the eels, tumbles; his toe is caught by a wolf, whose tail is in turn seized by an eagle, and so the chapter of accidents proceeds.

The difficulty of the ford being got over, our party continued their march towards Dol, which is here represented by a castle. The inscription is, ET VENERUNT AD DOL—And they came to Dol. The present town of Dol is a remarkable place, bearing thoroughly the aspect of ancient days. Its walls are tolerably perfect. However antique its walls and houses, its market presents us with traces of an antiquity greatly exceeding theirs. Large quantities of pottery, resembling in form and substance the commoner kinds used by the Romans, are here exposed for sale. It is curious to see Roman taste, as exhibited in such fragile articles, outliving the lapse of so many centuries.

As has been already stated, Conan intended to invade William, who, however, anticipated him. The Duke moreover came upon him unexpectedly, and found him engaged in settling a private quarrel with Rual, to whom the seigneury of the city of Dol belonged. The moment the forces of William made their appearance before the gates of Dol, Conan was constrained to flee, and take refuge in Rennes, the capital of Brittany. His army is represented in the Tapestry as fleeing to the city, pursued by the troops of the Norman Duke. Over this scene is the legend, ET CONAN FUGA VERTIT—And Conan betakes himself to flight.

Rual, the lord of Dol, was but little benefited by the retreat of Conan. William's forces scoured the country, and supplied their own wants at the expense of the inhabitants. Rual very politely thanked William for his deliverance, but hinted that if his army continued making such depredations everywhere, it was the same to him whether his country was ruined by Bretons or Normans. William issued orders prohibiting further devastation. A man is seen in the Tapestry letting himself down by a cord from the battlements of the castle; this, it has been conjectured, is the messenger sent to Duke William. A castle represents the city of Rennes, over which is inscribed the word REDNES.

We next meet with the town of Dinan. The inscription reads, HIC MILITES WILLELMI DUCIS PUGNANT CONTRA DINANTES—Here the soldiers of William attack Dinan. The place is undergoing all the calamities of a siege. Some of William's party are assailing it, but their onset is met by the exertions of the garrison. Others apply flames to the structure. We learn from the Tapestry that the castle was obliged to yield, and we see that the act of surrender is conducted in a very formal manner *(Plate IX)*. An inhabitant of the town, probably Conan himself, (ET CUNAN CLAVES PORREXIT—And Conan reached out the keys) is seen handing out the keys upon a lance, and they are received in a similar way by one of the chiefs of the attacking party. Both spears are adorned with a pennon or banner.[a] As we have no account of this siege in the chronicles, we can only gather its history from the stitches before us. Most likely William was satisfied with the formal submission of Conan, and quietly withdrew his forces. We do not in the Tapestry observe any of the invading troops entering the town.

Before proceeding further, we may notice some of the prominent

[a] It is often asserted that the house of Percy derived its name from one of the family having slain Malcolm, King of Scotland, by thrusting the spear into his eye when he came forward to demand the keys of Alnwick Castle. That historic name occurs in the Battle Abbey Roll, and is derived from the cradle of the family, the hamlet of Perci, in Normandy.

features of the castles which have been presented to our view. All of them are built upon elevated mounds. This was certainly one of the characteristics of an early Norman fortress. Further, we see that they were surrounded by a fosse, the section of which, in the Tapestry, is very boldly marked. In the case of Dinan, we have a barricade on the outside of this entrenchment. Besides these outworks, the castles consist of an outer fortification, or bailey, and of an interior building, or keep. The colouring of these structures may be purely fanciful, but I am disposed to think that the vertical stripes which we see upon some of them represent timber. The remains of some castles in Cornwall incontestably prove that, occasionally at least, the outside of the walls was braced with timber.[a] The walls of Guildford Castle are pierced with holes, which we are told were made for the scaffolding, and in order to hasten the drying of the mortar were left unfilled, and have since remained so. Is it not more likely that these cavities were formerly occupied by bolts for fastening an outside timber-casing to the walls?

But to proceed with Queen Matilda's narrative. The campaign in Brittany being brought to a satisfactory conclusion, the honours of knighthood awaited the Saxon Earl. William himself confers upon him the envied dignity. The superscription is HIC WILELMUS DEDIT

[a] The walls of Tintagel Castle " were evidently constructed in a framework of wood; the square holes which pierce the walls at regular intervals, from the foundations upwards, show the places once occupied by bond pieces, by which the wooden frames were held together."—*Notes by Rev. W. Haslam, in Report of Royal Inst. Cornwall,* 1850.

HAROLDO ARMA—Here William gave arms to Harold. Both parties are shown in the Tapestry armed cap-a-pie. Harold holds in his hand the banner which, by virtue of the rank now bestowed upon him, he is entitled to bear. William is seen placing with one hand the helmet on Harold's head, and with the other bracing the straps of his hauberk.

The Norman Duke, in conferring the honour of knighthood upon his adopted son in arms, doubtless exhorted him to fight valiantly in the cause of God and the ladies, and especially to bear himself gallantly against any one who should disparage the beauty of that one lady to whom he had plighted his troth. In this way William strengthened the meshes which he had already cast over Harold.

It has been noticed that the mode of conferring knighthood used on this occasion is a compromise between the Norman and Saxon methods. Ingulphus tells us that the ministrations of a priest were required when knighthood was conferred among the Saxons, but that the Normans regarded it entirely as a military ceremony.[a] Further, whilst the Normans, whose military strength lay in cavalry, performed the ceremony on horseback, the Saxons, who had no cavalry, always performed it on foot. In the case before us the ceremony is performed on foot, but without the agency of a priest. According to Wace, the ceremony of knighthood took place before the commencement of the campaign in Brittany. This is one of those variations which prove the independence of each authority.

[a] Ingulph's Chronicle (Bohn), p. 14.

William and Harold, who had been sojourning so long together, fighting side by side, living in the same tent, eating at the same board, now came to Bayeux (WILLELMVS VENIT BAGIAS—William came to Bayeux), and here the Saxon Earl came under that obligation the breach of which filled men's minds with horror and indignation. William could not but be aware that Harold intended to seize the crown of England on the death of the Confessor; he resolved therefore to avail himself of the present opportunity of throwing as many obstacles in his path as possible. Considering that Harold had come over professedly to announce to William that he was to be the successor to the Confessor, considering the very friendly terms on which they had now for some time been, and the very great obligations under which the Norman Duke had laid him, he could not refuse to take the oath. He no doubt felt, moreover, that he was in William's power, and knew full well that unless he complied with his demand he would not be allowed to return to his native shores. He therefore swore to support his rival's claims to the English throne. As the perjury of Harold was one of the pleas most successfully urged by William against his opponent, it invites our careful attention. Our faithful chronicler Wace gives us a full account of the transaction.—

" To receive the oath William caused a parliament to be called. It is commonly said that it was at Bayeux that he had his great council assembled. He sent for all the holy bodies thither, and put so many of them together as to fill a whole chest, and then covered them with a pall; but Harold neither saw them, nor knew of their being there; for nought was shown or told him about it; and over all was a philactery, the best that he could select...... When Harold placed his hand upon it, the hand trembled and the flesh quivered; but he swore and promised upon his oath to take Ele to wife, and to deliver up England to the Duke; and thereunto to do all in his power, according to his might and wit, after the death of Edward, if he should live, so help him God and the holy relics there! Many cried 'God grant it!' and when Harold had kissed the saints and had risen upon his feet, the Duke led him up to the chest and made him stand near it, and took off the chest the pall that had covered it, and showed Harold upon what holy relics he had sworn; he was sorely alarmed at the sight."[a]

In this account there is a little inconsistency. We are told of Harold's amazement when he had seen the relics, but we were previously informed that when he first placed his hand upon the chest "the hand trembled and the flesh quivered." If he did not know that dead men's bones were under the pall he must have suspected it; he must have known that this was the customary mode of taking an oath.[b]

---

[a] Taylor's Wace, p. 83.

[b] The Normans seem to have been particularly addicted to the worship of relics. They carried them about their persons, and had them enclosed in the handles of their swords. In the *Song of Roland* that hero is represented, when dying, as addressing his sword thus:—" Ah, Saint Durandal! in thy golden pommel what precious relics lie hid! A tooth of Saint Peter!—Blood of Saint Basil!—Hair of Monseigneur Saint Denis!—Vesture of the Virgin Mary! And shall a pagan possess thee?" Being thus at all times provided with relics, they were never at a loss as to the administration of an oath. In the Song already referred to we have a case in point:—' Be it as thou wilt,' answered Ganelon, and upon the relics of his sword he swore to the treason and consummated his crime."

In the Tapestry, Harold stands between two objects. One of them is a reliquary of the usual form, to which two staves are attached for the purpose of carriage. This reliquary has, however, a *superaltare* attached to it, such as is usually placed upon altars for the purpose of containing the consecrated wafer. The other object is an altar of the usual form and character. There does not seem to have been much temptation to William to practise a trick upon Harold, for he had so completely committed himself to the Duke that he could not avoid taking the oath, even though no covering had concealed the bones. But whether William did or did not practise this base artifice upon the Earl, it was natural that the Tapestry, being the work of Matilda, should endeavour to throw a veil over it. He is certainly in the Tapestry exhibited as swearing by the relics in the chest and by the host upon the altar, and he evidently touches them as if he knew they contained something very dreadful—he could not approach red-hot iron much more charily. We can readily conceive that after the ceremony William, by way of making as lively an impression as possible upon the mind of his victim, displayed the bones to him in all their sepulchral hideousness, and told them out in full tale before him. In such a case Harold might readily shrink from the exhibition, and be surprised at the number of martyrs which William's diligence had brought together. William was too brave a man to attempt the mean artifice which historians ascribe to him. Harold never accused him of it. When reminded before the battle of Hastings, by a messenger of the Duke's, of the oath he had taken, he sent this answer back, "Say to the Duke that I desire he will not remind me of my covenant nor of my oath; if I ever foolishly made it and promised him any thing, I did it for my liberty. I swore in order to get my freedom; whatever he asked I agreed to; and I ought not to be reproached, for I did nothing of my own free will."[a]

But after all, this oath of Harold's was not in the estimation of the men of that day the serious thing that has been represented. Men whom an oath taken in the name and in the presence of the living God could not bind, were not to be restrained by any moral influence. A little ingenuity only was requisite to release a man from an oath taken upon the relics. In the *Roman de Rou* we have a case in point.[b] At Val de Dunes the rebel lords of Normandy appeared in arms against the Duke. Before the opposing hosts joined, Raol Tesson, who was arrayed against William, was seen to act with hesitancy. His men besought him not to make war upon his lawful lord, whatever he did, reminding him that the man who would fight against his lord had no right to fief or barony. Raol could understand this argument, but what was he to do? he "had pledged himself, and sworn upon the saints at Bayeux to smite William wherever he should find him." The difficulty was however got over. Ordering his men to rest where they were, "he came spurring over the plain, struck his lord with his glove, and said laughingly to him, 'What I have sworn to do that I perform; I had sworn to

" Wace, p. 138.   b Wace, p. 20, 21.

IX. THE CASTLE OF DINAN SURRENDERS; WILLIAM KNIGHTS HAROLD AND THEY RIDE TO BAYEUX, WHERE HAROLD SWEARS

ALLEGIANCE TO THE DUKE.

X. HAROLD'S OATH TO DUKE WILLIAM OF NORMANDY.

XI. HAROLD RETURNS TO ENGLAND AND IS RECEIVED BY KING EDWARD.

XII. HAROLD AT THE COURT OF KING EDWARD.

XIII. THE DEATH AND FUNERAL OF EDWARD; HAROLD BECOMES KING OF ENGLAND.

XIV. THE CORONATION OF KING HAROLD.

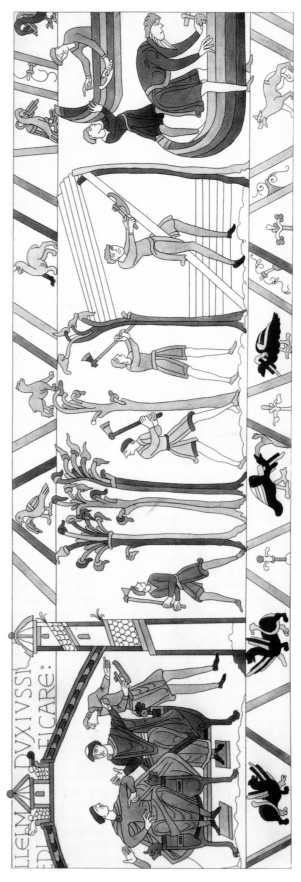

XV. NEWS REACHES WILLIAM OF HAROLD'S CORONATION; HE ORDERS THE CONSTRUCTION OF A FLEET FOR THE INVASION OF ENGLAND.

ᚼIC TRAhVNT:NAVES ADMAᚱE·

ᚼIC TRAhVNT:NAVES AD MAᚱE·

ISTI PORTANT:ARMAS:ADNAVES:ET hIC ᚻIC:WILLELM:DVX INᚱ
TRAhVNT:CARRVM
CVM VINO:ET ARMIS·

smite you as soon as I should find you; and as I would not perjure myself, I have now struck you to acquit myself of my oath, and henceforth I will do you no farther wrong or felony.' Then the Duke said, 'Thanks to thee!' and Raol thereupon went on his way back to his men." Success attended the side which Raol thus espoused, and we hear nothing of his perjury. Harold fell on the hard-fought field of Hastings, and heaven and earth resounded with cries of horror at the foul sin. Had he won, a new abbey, or the re-imposition of Peter's pence, would have cleared off the score.

Harold was now permitted to return home. The ship in which he sailed is represented in the Tapestry. Over the scene is the inscription, HIC HAROLD DUX REVERSUS EST AD ANGLICAM TERRAM— Here Harold the Earl returned to England. His approach to the shore is anxiously looked for by a watchman on the top of the gate-tower of his palace at Bosham. On reaching the land of his nativity Harold lost no time in repairing to court—ET VENIT AD EDWARDVM REGEM—And came to Edward the King. At the beginning of Plate VII. we see him in the presence of his sovereign, who reprimands him, as we have already observed (p. 28), for the miscarriage of his Commission.

V. THE SUCCESSION.

" Crowned but to die."——
Rogers.

THE latter days of Edward the Confessor were embittered by the prospect of those evils which he saw were coming upon England. On the Easter day before he died he held his court at Westminster. William of Malmesbury tells us that " While the rest were greedily eating, and making up for the long fast of Lent by the newly-provided viands, he was absorbed in the contemplation of some divine matter, when presently he excited the attention of the guests by bursting into profuse laughter." On earnest enquiry being made of him as to this unusual circumstance, he said " that the seven sleepers in Mount Cœlius, who had lain for two hundred years on their right side, had now turned upon their left; that they would continue to lie in this manner for seventy-four years, which would be a dreadful omen to wretched mortals. Nation would rise against nation, and kingdom against kingdom; earthquakes would be in divers places; pestilence and famine, terrors from heaven, and great signs; changes in kingdoms; wars of the gentiles against the Christians, and also victories of the Christians over the pagans."[a]

This was not the only vision he had. On one occasion he had

[a] William of Malmesbury, p. 249.

lain two days speechless; on the third, sadly and deeply sighing as he awoke from his torpor, he said, that two monks from Normandy whom he had known in his youth had appeared to him, and had spoken to the following effect:—" Since the chiefs of England, the dukes, bishops, and abbots, are not the ministers of God, but of the devil, God, after your death, will deliver this kingdom for a year and a day into the hands of the enemy, and devils shall wander over all the land."[a]

Borne down by these painful anticipations, Edward rapidly sank. Feeling death approach, he hastened the completion of the abbey church of Westminster, in which he designed that his body should be laid. He lived to realize this his last care. Roger of Wendover says, " Edward King of England, held his court at Christmas (1065) at Westminster; and, on the blessed Innocents' day, caused the church which he had erected from its foundations, outside the city of London, to be dedicated with great pomp in honour of St. Peter, the prince of the apostles; but both before and during the solemn festival of this dedication, the King was confined with severe illness." At length " the pacific King Edward, the glory of England, the son of King Ethelred, exchanged a temporal for an eternal kingdom, in the fourth indiction, on the vigil of our Lord's Epiphany, being the fifth day of the week. The day after his death the most blessed King was buried at London, in the church which he himself had built in a new and costly style of architecture, which was afterwards adopted by numbers."[b]

[a] Malmesbury, p. 252.   [b] Vol. i. p. 322.

The Tapestry exhibits to us the church of St. Peter at Westminster, and the funeral procession of the recently departed
monarch. The church is a building of the Norman style in its
greatest simplicity. As is usual in cathedrals and conventual
churches of the first class, it has its tower in the centre, and is
provided with transepts. The weathercock may perhaps excite
attention, as proving that this appendage of our churches is no
novelty. It appears in the Saxon illustrations of Cædmon. But
what is particularly worthy of our notice is, that a workman
appears to be in the act of affixing it. By this, the designer of
the Tapestry means to show that the church was but just completed when the interment of the Confessor took place. A hand
appears over the western end of the church to denote the finger of
Providence, and to indicate that it was the will of God that the
remains of the departed King should be deposited in that building.
A similar hand appears on the coins of some of the Roman emperors, and in several of the sculptures of the catacombs at Rome.
This is another indication that the artist was acquainted with the
Roman method of treating such subjects.

We next meet with the funeral of the King. The circumstance
which chiefly strikes us in it is its simplicity. No gilded cross is
borne before the body. No candles, lighted or unlighted, are
carried in procession. The attendants, clerical and lay, wear their
ordinary dresses. Two youths go by the side of the bier, ringing
bells. That the persons who follow the bearers are ecclesiastics is
evident from their shaven crowns. Two of them have books, from

which they chant some requiem. Only one of them has a mantle, betokening him to be a person of importance. The body, agreeably to the Saxon custom, has been wound up in a cloth, fastened with transverse bandages.[a] It is carried head-foremost. At a date not long subsequent to the Conquest it was usual to carry the bodies of princes to the grave fully exposed to view, dressed in all the habiliments of state. The body, on arriving at the place of sepulture, would be deposited in the stone coffin that was prepared to receive it.[b] The legend here is, HIC PORTATUR CORPUS EADWARDI REGIS AD ECCLESIAM SANCTI PETRI APOSTOLI— Here the body of King Edward is carried to the church of St. Peter the Apostle.

On proceeding to the next compartment we are surprised at being introduced into the chamber of the dying King, whose remains we have already seen conducted to the grave. Some writers think that here the artist has been guilty of an oversight, or that the fair ladies who carried out his design have been very inattentive to their instructions. The seeming inconsistency is very easily explained. A new subject is now entered upon, and that

[a] " Having first washed the corpse, it was clothed in a straight linen garment, or put into a bag or sack of linen, and then wrapped closely round from head to foot with a strong cloth wrapper."—*Strutt*, vol. i., p. 66.

[b] The custom of carrying the dead in some slight envelope to the sarcophagus which was to be its last resting place, accounts for the mischance which occurred at the burial of William the Conqueror, force being required to thrust the body into its too narrow cell. Bede tells us (*Ecc. Hist.* b. iv. c. xi.) how the stone coffin for Sebba, King of the East Saxons, was too small, and when the attendants were for bending the knees of the corpse a miracle ensued, and the coffin elongated of itself.

subject is the right of succession. One important element in it is the grant of the King. The historian of the Tapestry, in discussing this very important part of his design, found it necessary to revert to the scenes which preceded the death of the Confessor, and to the directions which in his last moments he had given.

The narrative which Wace gives us of the last hours of the King agrees well with the Tapestry. "The day came that no man can escape, and King Edward drew near to die. He had it much at heart that William should have his kingdom, if possible; but he was too far off, and it was too long to tarry for him, and Edward could not defer his hour. He lay in heavy sickness, in the illness whereof he was to die; and he was very weak, for death pressed hard upon him. Then Harold assembled his kindred, and sent for his friends and other people, and entered into the King's chamber, taking with him whomsoever he pleased. An Englishman began to speak first, as Harold had directed him, and said, 'Sire, we sorrow greatly that we are about to lose thee; and we are much alarmed, and fear that great trouble may come upon us. No heir of thine remains who may comfort us after thy death. ...... On this account the people weep and cry aloud, and say they are ruined, and that they shall never have peace again, if thou failest them. And in this I trow they say truly; for without a king they will have no peace, and a king they cannot have, save through thee. ...... Behold the best of thy people, the noblest of thy friends; all are come to beseech thee, and thou must grant their prayer before thou goest hence, or thou wilt not see God.

All come to implore thee that Harold may be King of this land. We can give thee no better advice, and no better canst thou do.' As soon as he had named Harold, all the English in the chamber cried out that he said well, and that the King ought to give heed to him. 'Sire!' they said, 'if thou dost it not we shall never in our lives have peace.' Then the King sat up in his bed, and turned his face to the English there, and said, 'Seigniors! you well know, and have oft-times heard, that I have given my realm at my death to the Duke of Normandy; and as I have given it, so have some among you sworn that it shall go.' But Harold, who stood by, said, 'Whatever thou hast heretofore done, sire! consent now that I shall be King, and that your land be mine. I wish for no other title, and want no one to do any thing more for me.' So the King turned round and said, whether of his own free will I know not,—'Let the English make either the Duke or Harold king, as they please; I consent.' So he let the barons have their own will."[a] This narrative bears all the marks of probability, and is quite consistent with the representations of the Tapestry. The circumstance of the dying monarch's having been clamorously assailed, at a time when peace is most required, by the adherents of Harold, in order to induce him to alter the arrangements he had already made respecting the succession, was calculated to win for the Duke the sympathy of all right-minded persons.

Still, the question remains, why should Harold have been so anxious to be nominated the successor of the Confessor?

[a] Wace, p. 89.

Three circumstances seem to have constituted a legal claim to the throne among the Anglo-Saxons—heirship, the appointment of the departed monarch, and the election of the nobles.

That heirship alone did not constitute a valid claim to the throne is plain from the will of King Alfred, which has been preserved by Asser. He there styles himself king of the whole of Wessex, by the consent of the nobility, *nobilitatis consensu pariter et assensu rex;* and in the same public act declares that he inherited the kingdom, after his two brothers Ethelbald and Ethelred, by the will of his father, *de hereditate, quam pater meus Ethelwulphus ...... delegavit.* It is quite evident, therefore, that a thoroughly valid claim to the crown was of the triple nature now represented. As neither Harold nor William belonged to the royal line of England, the remaining sources of right became of the more importance to them.

Let us now revert to the Tapestry. The feeble condition of the King is well represented. An attendant is supporting him behind with a pillow, whilst he makes an attempt to speak. The blackness of death has settled upon his shrunken countenance. A priest dressed in canonicals stands by, whose uplifted hand and sorrow-stricken face seem to say that the grand climax is at hand. A lady at the foot of the bed weeps; she is doubtless the wife of the Confessor, the sister of Harold. Harold is eagerly pressing his claim. The legend here is, HIC EADWARDUS REX IN LECTO ALLO-QUIT: FIDELES—Here King Edward on his bed addresses his faithful attendants. Underneath is a scene, which the inscription explains,

ET HIC DEFUNCTUS EST—And here he is dead. A priest in canonicals is again present, probably the one we saw above, and two attendants wrap up the body for burial.

The compartment before us is the only one in the Tapestry in which two scenes are given in one breadth. This is probably not without design. The death and burial of Edward, and the election and coronation of Harold, all took place within eight-and-forty hours. It was of great importance to Harold to get actual possession of the crown before William could put in his claim. It was usual in these times to perform the ceremonies of coronation only at one of the great festivals of the church. Edward died on the last day but one of Christmas, and for Harold to wait till Easter, the next festival, was to throw away the important advantage which he had gained over his rival. Hence the rapidity with which the coronation of Harold followed the death of the Confessor. It is to show, that no sooner had the vital spirit fled than preparations for the burial were begun, that we have the two scenes in the same compartment.

The next pictures represent the election and coronation of Harold. William of Malmesbury says, " While the grief for the King's death was yet fresh, Harold, on the very day of the Epiphany, seized the diadem, and extorted from the nobles their consent; though the English say, that it was granted him by the King."

In many respects the Tapestry is more candid than the Chroniclers. It here says, HIC DEDERUNT HAROLDO CORONAM REGIS— Here they gave the crown of the King to Harold; and the next legend is, HIC RESIDET HAROLD REX ANGLORUM—Here is seated Harold, King of the English. One contemporary writer denies that Harold was anointed at all, or had any claim but his own usurpation. In the Doomsday Survey, Harold is mentioned as seldom as possible, and when his name does occur it is not as King Harold, but Harold the Earl. The Norman chroniclers, writing subsequently to the time when William had established his conquest, seldom write his name without appending some derogatory epithet to it, such as "the perfidious and perjured King Harold." All this seems to favour the idea that the Tapestry was designed during the first visit of William to Normandy. He had not then broken faith with the Saxon nobles who thronged his court; he was not yet independent of their good will, so that in stating his own claims to the crown, he found it necessary not entirely to ignore their views. After he was firmly established, he cared not what women stitched or clerks wrote.

The artist has managed the election-scene very adroitly. One nobleman, in the name of the people, offers Harold the crown, which, as he intimates by the finger directed towards the death-scene of Edward, he has just taken from the head of that monarch. Harold looks most wistfully at it. He seems to say—I should like very much to have it, but I know it does not belong to me. For a moment he forbears to extend his hand to grasp it. His right elbow is towards it, but his hand remains upon his belt. On a line with the crown is an axe, held by another nobleman, somewhat significantly turned towards Harold. Harold has his own axe in his left hand, and it too, though apparently by accident, is turned towards himself. The Norman artist, in thus managing the subject, manifestly serves the cause of William better than if he had altogether disowned the fact of Harold's election.

That Harold should have been elected by the people is nothing wonderful. The native population had groaned under the domination of a crowd of foreigners, brought over by Edward the Confessor. They must have felt that under William, a Norman by lineage as well as education, the evil would be perpetuated and increased. Hence they gave their voices most cordially and unanimously for the Saxon. Most of the English chroniclers distinctly state, that Harold was duly elected to the office by the nobles. Thus Roger of Hoveden, following Florence of Worcester, writes, " After his burial, the Viceroy Harold, son of Earl Godwin, whom before his decease the king had appointed his successor, was elevated to the throne by all the chief men of England, and was on the same day, with due honour, consecrated king."[a] That Harold did not thrust himself upon the people, is abundantly proved by the fact that not one man of Saxon blood deserted him upon the landing of William.

In our days the great reason which rendered a strictly hereditary succession to the crown inexpedient does not exist. The adoption of that wise maxim that a monarch can only rule by his ministers, renders the personal qualifications of the monarch of less importance than in former days. Still, even in our time, a remnant exists of the ancient form of election. In the coronation service

[a] Annals of Roger de Hoveden, vol. i. p. 130.

M

the king is directed, after entering the church and attending to his private devotions, to take his seat, not on the throne, but on the chair before and below the throne, and there repose himself. Then the first part of the service, called the " Recognition," is to be proceeded with. In it the archbishop, accompanied by the great officers of state, severally addresses the assembly northwards and southwards, eastwards and westwards, saying, with a loud voice, the king meanwhile standing up, " Sirs ! I here present unto you ——the undoubted king of this realm : wherefore all of you who are come this day to do your homage, are you willing to do the same ?" It is not until the people, thus severally addressed, have signified their assent by crying out, " God save the king !" that the ceremony is proceeded with.

Harold, though he well knew the dangers attending the step, accepted the crown. Few could have rejected the tempting offer. He was moreover a brave man, and thoroughly imbued with Saxon feeling. He was willing to peril his life for the national peculiarities of his country. He was accordingly straightway anointed, and the Tapestry next exhibits him seated upon his throne, manifesting all the pomp and dignity of a king. The throne is considerably elevated above the floor of the apartment. The sceptre is in one hand, the ball in the other. His officers present him with the sword of justice. On his left hand stands Stigand, in his archiepiscopal robes. The superscription calls him Stigant, which seems further to show that the artist was not an Englishman. Wace the chronicler, who was a Norman, usually calls Harold,

Heraut. The inscription gives Stigand his title of Archbishop—
ARCHIEPS, a contraction for ARCHIEPISCOPUS. At a period later
than that in which we have supposed the Tapestry to have been
prepared, he would not have been so denominated. For a variety
of reasons Stigand was distasteful to the authorities of Rome. For
some years prior to the Conquest, the payment of Peter's pence
had been discontinued, and Stigand, in common with all Englishmen, was looked upon coldly. Stigand, moreover, had succeeded
the Norman archbishop, Robert de Jumieges, who had been ex-
pelled the country in the rising under Godwin. The Normans
were at this time better churchmen than the English. Stigand
further, in common with the majority of the Saxon clergy, was an
advocate of " the older doctrine of the eucharist;" Lanfranc, who
superseded him, was, in common with the authorities at Rome, an
ardent maintainer of the doctrine of transubstantiation. Under all
these circumstances, Stigand, on being made archbishop of Canterbury by the Confessor, was not very sanguine of having the
appointment confirmed by the Pope, and instead of making an
immediate application to Rome, quietly took possession of the *pallium*, which his predecessor in his haste had left behind him. At
length he did apply, and Benedict X., for reasons arising out of
his own peculiar position, granted him the *pallium*. This, however,
only made matters worse. Benedict X. was speedily dethroned
by an army from beyond the mountains, and a new pope elected,
who excommunicated his predecessor and annulled all his acts.
Stigand, therefore, found himself once more without the *pallium*,

accused of usurpation, and charged with a new and much more serious crime, that of having solicited the favour and countenance of a false and excommunicated pope. If the Tapestry had been constructed after Lanfranc had planted his foot upon the necks of the English clergy, Stigand would not have been denominated archbishop. When William of Malmesbury has occasion to name him, he calls him " the pretended and false archbishop."

The Norman chroniclers, for the most part, agree with the Tapestry in stating that Harold was crowned by Stigand, archbishop of Canterbury. Florence of Worcester and Roger of Hoveden state, that the solemn ceremony was performed by Aldred, Archbishop of York. Roger of Wendover says that the King " placed the diadem on his own head."

The dress of the archbishop nearly resembles that of a Roman Catholic prelate of the present day. The *stole* will be observed. The *pallium*, which subsequently was made of pure white wool, is in Stigand's case purple.[a] The *maniple* which, at a later period was worn upon the arm of the priest, is in the Tapestry, and other contemporaneous drawings, placed on the wrist. But the circumstance most observable in the costume of Stigand is the absence of the mitre. This distinctive decoration of the episcopal office seems not to have been known at this period. It is not met with in the Catacombs of Rome. In the illustrations of the *Benedictional of St. Æthelwold* we have priests and apostles in

---

[a] The *paludamentum*, or official dress of a Roman general, to which the episcopal *pallium* is probably to be traced, was either of a brilliant white, scarlet, or purple colour.

great numbers, but none of them wear a mitre, unless the circle round the head of St. Benedict be one. The same remark applies to the illustrations of the metrical *Paraphrase* of Cædmon. The bishops of the Lewes chess-men, which seem to have been executed about the middle of the twelfth century, probably furnish us with the earliest British examples of a mitre. The mitres worn by the ecclesiastics who support the head of the sovereign on the tomb of King John, at Worcester, are also early examples.[a]

In an apartment next to that in which the ceremonies of the coronation are being solemnized several spectators are assembled, expressing by their gestures surprise and apprehension. In the spring of the year 1066 an event occurred which filled the minds of men with alarm. At Easter a comet appeared, which is noticed by nearly all the chroniclers. Wace thus describes it:—"Now while these things were doing a great star appeared, shining for fourteen days, with three long rays streaming towards the earth; such a star as is wont to be seen when a kingdom is about to change its king. I have seen many men who saw it, men of full age at the time, and who lived many years after. Those who would discourse of the stars call it a comet." Our worsted astronomers have produced a very brilliant meteor, with more than twice three streams of fire issuing from it. Fear doubtless proved a multiplying glass in their hands. This drawing is, however, remarkable, as furnishing us with the earliest representation that we have of these erratic bodies.

[a] See note D, at the end of the volume.

The discoveries of modern science have attached a peculiar degree of interest to this comet. Halley, the astronomer, having noticed that a brilliant comet had been seen in the years 1531, 1607 and 1682, conceived the idea that it was the same body which had appeared on these several occasions, and ventured to affirm that comets, like the other heavenly objects with which we are acquainted, obeyed the laws of gravitation. The reappearance of this comet in 1759 established his position, and proved that its periodic time was about seventy-seven years. These facts, together with the subsequent accurate calculation of the orbit of the body, enable us to carry back our reckonings, so as to render it highly probable that the comet which alarmed our ancestors is that which bears the name of Halley, and whose return in the year 1835 was looked forward to by the civilized world with so much delightful anticipation. Mr. Hinde, in his recently published book on Comets, says, " There is considerable probability in favour of the appearance of the comet in the year of the Norman conquest, or in April 1066. This famous body, which astonished Europe in that year, is minutely, though not very clearly, described in the Chinese annals, and its path, there assigned, is found to agree with elements which have great resemblance to those of Halley's comet ...... It was equal to the full moon in size, and its train, at first short, increased to a wonderful length. Almost every historian and writer of the eleventh century bears witness to the splendour of the comet of 1066, in which we are disposed to recognise the comet of Halley."[a]

[a] Hinde on Comets, p. 52.

The legend to this part of the Tapestry is, ISTI MIRANT STELLAM —These men wonder at the star.

The minds of men were not long kept in suspense. The next compartment exhibits King Harold seated on his throne, bending down his ear very eagerly to a messenger who has arrived with important intelligence. The nature of it is explained by the dreamy-like flotilla which is shown in the lower border.

Harold, on succeeding to the throne, neglected to dispossess of their offices the Norman favourites whom Edward left behind him. He no doubt thought, by conciliation, to procure their good will. He was mistaken. A ship is immediately fitted out, and messengers sent to Normandy to acquaint the Duke with the important events which had just transpired. This is shown in the Tapestry *(Plate XV.)* in a scene which is superscribed, HIC NAVIS ANGLICA VENIT IN TERRAM WILLELMI DUCIS—Here an English ship came to the territory of Duke William.

William takes the news in terrible dudgeon. We see him in the next compartment sitting erect upon his ducal throne wearing an air of great indignation. His mantle seems to have partaken of the passion of its wearer, and is expanded to its full dimensions.

Wace tells us, " The Duke was in his park in Rouen. He held in his hand a bow, which he had strung and bent, making it ready for the arrow ...... when, behold ! ...... a serjeant appeared, who came journeying from England ...... who went straight to the Duke, and told him privily that King Edward was dead, and that Harold was raised to be king. When the Duke had listened to him ...... he became as a man enraged, and left the craft of the woods. Oft he tied his mantle, and oft he untied it again; and spoke to no man, neither dared any man speak to him. Then he crossed the Seine in a boat, and came to his hall and entered therein; and sat down at the end of a bench, shifting his place from time to time, covering his face with his mantle, and resting his head against a pillar. Thus he remained long, in deep thought, for no one dared to speak to him; but many asked aside, 'what ails the Duke? why makes he such bad cheer?'"

Once, in more recent history, a man standing on the shores of France was similarly agitated. Napoleon had ordered his fleets to the West Indies, in order that they might lead Nelson into a pursuit, and suddenly returning gain possession of the English Channel. Long and anxiously did he watch the signals which were to tell him that his point was gained—but he saw them not. When it was hinted that Villeneuve, instead of forcing his way to Brest, might possibly have steered for Cadiz, he gave way to successive gusts of passion, and read and re-read the despatches of of Villeneuve and of Lauriston. When told, at last, that beyond a doubt Villeneuve was at Cadiz, strong excesses of passion again ensued, and the Army of England was transferred from the heights of Boulogne to the plains of Austerlitz.

VI. PREPARATIONS.

"Curate, ut splendor meo sit clypeo clarior,
    Quam solis radii esse olim, quum sudum 'st, solent :
Ut, ubi usus veniat, contra conserta manu,
    Præstringat oculorum aciem in acie hostibus."
                                                Plautus.

THE Duke of Normandy was a bold man, and was not disposed to attempt any thing that he was not prepared to pursue to the end. He knew that Harold, with the power of England at his disposal, was no despicable enemy, and he resolved to fortify his cause in every possible way. The sea was to him an object of great dread, as he knew it would be to his followers. "If," he said, "he could attack and punish them without crossing the sea, he would willingly have done so; but he would rather cross the sea than not revenge himself and pursue his right."

William sent messengers to Harold demanding the crown, and reminding him of his oath. He would not have done this had he lost any time by it. Harold's reply was worthy of a constitutional monarch. "It is true that I took an oath to William; but I took it under constraint. I promised what did not belong to me; a promise which I could not in any way perform. My royal authority is not my own; I could not lay it down against the will of my country; nor can I, against the will of the country, take a foreign

N

wife."[a]   William referred the case to the Pope.   Harold, conscious that he was acting inconsistently with his oath, fearing that the cause would not be impartially heard, or not choosing to submit the destinies of England to the decision of a foreigner, made no appeal to the Holy Father.   The result of William's application was, that the Pope " granted his request, and sent him a gonfanon, and a very precious, rich, and fair ring, which, he said, had under the stone one of St. Peter's hairs.   With these tokens he commanded, and in God's name granted to him, that he should conquer England, and hold it of St. Peter."[b]

William, however, relied neither upon the tenderness of Harold's conscience nor upon the Pope's sense of justice—he looked mainly to his barons and retainers.   He summoned all who owed him suit and service to meet him in his castle at Lillebone.   He there opened to them his design of invading England, and urged them to double for this occasion the amount of their usual contributions of men and money.   The account given of this meeting affords us a good idea of the noisy nature of the parliaments of that day—a feature which they still occasionally exhibit.   " They remained long in council, and the debate lasted a great while ; for they hesitated long among themselves what they should say, what answer they should give, and what aid they would afford.   They complained much to each other, saying that they had been often aggrieved ; and they murmured much, conferring together in small parties ; here five, there fifteen, here forty, there thirty, sixty, a

[a] Thierry, p. 60.   [b] Taylor's Wace.

hundred. Some said they feared the sea, and were not bound to serve beyond it. Some said they were willing to bring ships and cross the sea with the Duke ; others said that they would not go, for they owed much, and were poor. Some would, others would not, and there was great contention among them."

William on this occasion acted upon his usual maxim, " divide and conquer." He dealt privately with such as he was most likely to influence, and having induced them to enter zealously into his plans, others were led by shame or sympathy to follow. He was lavish of his promises. To the barons he proffered numerous manors, to the clerks he held out the bait of rich benefices ; to these who were amorously inclined he promised wives with ample dowries ; to such as were not to be allured by prospective advantages he gave at once large sums of money. It is said that he offered much more than he could possibly perform ; for he was well aware that the Saxon battle-axes would cancel many of his bonds. Meanwhile the Pope's sanction of the scheme arrived in Normandy, and it inspired the invading hosts with fresh zeal. " The Duke rejoiced greatly at receiving the gonfanon, and the license which the Apostle [Pope] gave him. He got together carpenters, smiths, and other workmen ; so that great stir was seen in all the ports of Normandy, in the collecting of wood and materials, cutting of planks, framing of ships and boats, stretching sails, and rearing masts, with great pains and at great cost. They spent all one summer and autumn in fitting up the fleet and collecting the forces ; and there was no knight in the land, no good serjeant, archer, nor peasant of stout heart, and of age for battle, that the Duke did not summon to go with him to England."

The Tapestry represents these preparations. In the compartment which we last noticed William is accompanied by his half-brother Odo, who is busily employed in issuing orders to the master carpenter. This functionary holds a peculiarly shaped axe in his hand, of which there are some examples in the illustrations to *Cædmon's Paraphrase*. The superscription is, HIC WILLELM DUX JUSSIT NAVES EDIFICARE—Here Duke William issues orders for the building of ships.

Next we see the execution of the orders. Trees are being felled, and the planks prepared. Presently the ships have assumed their proper shape, and then we see them being drawn down to the shore. This operation is effected by means of a rope passed through a pulley inserted in a post driven into the shore below the water mark. The legend is HIC TRAHUNT NAVES AD MARE—Here they draw the vessels to the sea. Afterwards the stores and ammunition are taken on board, and when all is ready the horses and troops embark.

This may be a fitting place in which to introduce some observations upon the ships and armour of the Normans.

The vessels of this period were of small burden. This is proved by the fact that they were drawn down to the sea, after being built, in the manner shown in the Tapestry. The *Domesday Book* establishes the same thing. There we find it stated that Dover and Sandwich (and probably the other Cinque Ports also) were severally obliged to furnish the King with twenty ships for fifteen days, once every year, each vessel having a crew of twenty-one persons.[a] The gunwale of the vessels was low. In the Tapestry *(Plate XX)* we see them landing the horses, by making them leap over the sides of the ships on to the shore. On the voyage the gunwale was practically heightened by placing the shields of the soldiers along the sides of the vessel, one shield partly lying over another. The prow and stern of the ships, which are the same in form, are a good deal elevated, and are usually decorated with the head of a dragon, lion, bull, or some fanciful figure. We have several descriptions of the ship in which William sailed on his ever-memorable expedition. Wace says, "The Duke placed a lantern on the mast of his ship, that the other ships might see it, and hold their course after it. At the summit was a vane of brass gilt. On the head of the ship, in the front which mariners call the prow, there was a figure of a child in brass, bearing an arrow with a bended bow. His face was turned towards England, and thither he looked, as though he was about to shoot."[b] In an ancient MS. preserved in the British Museum, and printed in the Appendix of Lyttleton's *Henry II.*,[c] we are told that this figure pointed towards England with his right fore-finger, and held to his mouth an ivory horn with his left hand. With this description the Tapestry nearly agrees; the figure is, however, placed not on the prow, but at the stern of the vessel. The lamp would only be required

[a] Sir N. Harris Nicolas' Hist. Royal Navy, vol. i., p. 24.
[b] Wace, p. 123. [c] Vol. i., p. 464.

at night. On the top of the mast of William's vessel the sacred banner given him by the Pope is fixed, surmounted by a cross. The banner, as it appears here and in other parts of the Tapestry, would be described by heralds as "*argent*, a cross *or* in a bordure *azure*." The vessels have one mast, which is lowered forward as the land is approached. To the mast, supported by a few shrouds, or rather stays, a large square sail is suspended. The modern rudder was not known for some time after the period of the Conquest;[a] the vessels are steered by a paddle fixed to the quarter. The steersman, who was also the captain and pilot, holds the paddle in one hand, and the sheet in the other. This was exactly the position of Palinurus in the *Æneid* of Virgil.

"Ipse sedens clavumque regit, velisque ministrat."

The larger vessels of the ancients were provided with two paddle rudders, one on each quarter. This arrangement is shown in the recently-discovered sculptures of Nineveh and in many Roman coins. The ship in which St. Paul was wrecked on the shore of Malta had two rudders. The vessels in the Tapestry have only one paddle, pro-

"[a] This mode of steering was retained till a comparatively late period. In a bass-relief over the doorway of the leaning tower of Pisa, built in the twelfth century, ships are represented with paddle rudders, as those in the Bayeux Tapestry representing the Norman Invasion. They must have been in use till after the middle of the thirteenth century; for in the contracts to supply Louis IX. with ships, the contractors are bound to furnish them with two rudders. By the middle of the following century we find the hinged rudders on the gold noble of Edward III. The change in the mode of steering must, therefore, have taken place about the end of the thirteenth, or early in the fourteenth, century."—*Smith's Voyage and Shipwreck of St. Paul.*

bably on account of their inferior size. It is perhaps worthy of the consideration of modern navigators, whether, in cases where the hinged rudder is displaced in a storm, the paddle-rudder might not advantageously be resorted to as a temporary expedient. The anchors of the Tapestry resemble those in modern use. The anchor of the ship in which the spies of William sail to Normandy *(Plate XV.)* has no stock—but this is probably merely an oversight of the draftsman, for in an earlier case *(Plate II.)* the stock is represented.

The sides of the ships are painted of various colours in longitudinal stripes, each stripe probably representing a plank. The sails of the ships are also variously coloured. Roger of Wendover tells us that the Conqueror's ship had a crimson sail; probably this is nearly correct, for in the Tapestry it is painted red, with a yellow stripe in the middle.

The effect of the whole fleet must have been very striking, and well calculated to make a powerful impression upon spectators of that or any age.

Writers differ much as to the number of the vessels in William's fleet, as well as of the men they carried. Wace says, " I heard my father say—I remember it well, though I was but a lad—that there were seven hundred ships less four, when they sailed from St. Valeri; and that there were, besides these, ships' boats and skiffs for the purpose of carrying harness. I have found it written (but I know not whether it be true) that there were in all three thousand vessels bearing sails and masts. Any one will know that there must have been a great many men to have furnished out so many vessels."

The different computations of the chroniclers probably arise from some of them including the small transport vessels in their reckoning and others not. Most modern historians set down William's army at sixty thousand strong. The transport of so large a body of troops would require a flotilla more numerous than had sailed upon any waters since the decline of the Roman empire.

The armour of the combatants in the Tapestry may now engage our attention.

Nearly all the combatants are provided with helmets. The precise shape of them we learn from those which are being brought to the shore to be placed with other military stores on board the fleet. The helmet has a conical form, and is provided with a projection in front called the nasal, to protect the face. In some of them there appears to be a smaller projection at the back. It is a remarkable circumstance that exceedingly few helmets have been found in the graves of the Franks and Saxons, which are usually replete with military implements. Two however have been found in this country, one near Cheltenham the other in Derbyshire.[a] From these specimens, as well as from the appearance of those in the Tapestry, we may suppose that the helmet consisted of a framework of iron, over which a covering of leather was stretched. From the fact, however, that so few helmets have been found in Saxon graves, we may perhaps infer that the framework of the

[a] They are engraved in Smith's Collectanea Antiqua, vol. ii., p. 238.

earlier specimens was of wood. Wace makes express mention of one man who at the battle of Hastings wore a wooden helmet:— " On the other side (he says) was an Englishman who much annoyed the French, assaulting them with a keen-edged hatchet. He had a helmet made of wood, which he had fastened down to his coat and laced round his neck, so that no blows could reach his head. The ravage he was making was seen by a gallant Norman knight, who rode a horse that neither fire nor water could stop in its career when its lord urged it on. The knight spurred, and his horse carried him on till he charged the Englishman, striking him over the helmet, so that it fell down over his eyes; and as he stretched out his hand to raise it and uncover his face, the Norman cut off his right hand, so that his hatchet fell to the ground. Another Norman sprung forward, and eagerly seized the prize with both his hands, but he kept it little space and paid dearly for it; for as he stooped to pick up the hatchet, an Englishman with his long-handled axe struck him over the back, breaking all his bones, so that his entrails and lungs gushed forth. The knight of the good horse meantime retired without injury."[a]

The helmet speedily underwent several changes after the period of the battle of Hastings. Flaps were affixed to the sides in order to protect the ears and the cheeks. These appear in the chess-men found in the island of Lewis, which, as already observed, belong to a period not later than the middle of the twelfth century. Soon after the Conquest the nasal being found to be inconvenient was

[a] Wace, p. 210.

O

frequently omitted; at length the contrivance called the *ventaille* was introduced, which when brought over the face fully protected it, and yet, as its name implies, admitted air to the nostrils of the wearer, and when his convenience required could be lifted up. That the *ventaille* was not known at the battle of Hastings appears from the helmets which are being taken on board the fleet. Another fact represented on the Tapestry *(Plate XXX.)* shows the same thing; William, when he wishes to show himself in order to contradict the rumour that he has been killed, is obliged to lift his helmet almost off his head. And yet Wace, who lived at the period just subsequent to the Conquest, writes as though Harold's helmet was provided with a *ventaille*. He says, "Harold was sorely wounded in his eye by the arrow, and suffered grievous pain from the blow. An armed man came in the throng of the battle and struck him on the *ventaille* of his helmet, and beat him to the ground." This passage shows how exceedingly difficult it is, when describing past events, to avoid anachronisms. Sir Samuel Meyrick, in commenting upon this passage, says, "By the *ventaille* is here meant merely the open part below his helmet. The *ventaculum*, or *ventaille*, strictly speaking, was not invented at this time, but was in full use when Wace lived; he adopts it therefore merely for the sake of the rhyme, and as familiar to his countrymen." [a]

The body armour consisted of a tunic of leather or stout linen, on which was fastened some substance calculated to resist the stroke of a weapon. Occasionally, as we have already seen, over-

[a] Crit. Inquiry into Ancient Armour, vol. i., p. 8.

lapping flaps of leather, sometimes pieces of horn or horses' hoofs, and not unfrequently plates or rings of iron were employed. When rings were used they were laid side by side, and not locked into each other, as was the case in the chain armour of a subsequent date. When small plates of iron were used they were generally lozenge-shaped; hence this species of armour has been termed mascled. The ingenuity of man has had recourse to these and similar contrivances in every age. Amongst the ruins of Nineveh scale armour has been discovered, and on Trajan's column the Sarmatian cavalry and their horses are clad in it.

The coat of mail comprehended body, legs, and arms all in one piece; the legs and arms were however short and loose. It is difficult to understand the mode of putting it on. It seems to have been drawn over the head. We are expressly told that when William was preparing for the battle he had his hauberk brought; but in *putting his head in*, to get it on, he inadvertently turned it the wrong way, with the back part in front;" and that seeing his error, "he crossed himself, *stooped his head*, and put it on aright." In the Tapestry *(Plate XXXII.)* we see some persons stripping the slain; they uniformly draw the hauberk over the head. The legs of the dress must in this case have been made to open. When on, it was tightened by straps at the breast. This armour seems to have been occasionally provided with a hood of the same material, which covered the head. There are some examples of it in the Tapestry. The legs in the Tapestry are for the most part left unprotected; occasionally they are wrapped round

with bandages of leather; in the case of a few of the leading personages they are covered with mascled or ring armour. The weight
of the hauberk, or haubergeon, must have been considerable. In
taking the dresses down to the ships we observe two men are
employed to carry one; they bear it on a pole upon their shoulders.
One of William's nobles, whilst waiting at Hastings for the onset
of Harold, complained of the weight of his armour. The Duke
quietly desired him to put it off, and then putting it on himself
over his own hauberk, mounted his horse without assistance, and
rode off, to the great chagrin of the noble and the astonishment of all.[a]

The shields of the ancient knights formed an important part of
their equipment. The shield of the early Saxons was circular,
having a boss in the centre. The boss was concave on the inside
of the shield, and of a size sufficient to contain the hand of the
warrior, which grasped the shield by a handle put across the
cavity. In the Tapestry we have some examples of the circular
shield, but by far the larger part of the shields on the Saxon as
well as the Norman side are of a different character. It would
appear that the intercourse subsisting between Normandy and England during the reign of the Confessor had led to the abandonment

[a] When Harold, in 1063, conducted an expedition against the Welch, he found
the heavy armour of his troops unsuitable to the service on which they were engaged, and immediately changed it. Ingulf says, "Seeing that the activity of the
Welch proved remarkably effective against the more cumbrous movements of the
English, and that, after making an attack, they retreated into the woods, while our
soldiers, being weighed down with their arms, were unable to follow them, he ordered
all his soldiers to accustom themselves to wear armour made of boiled leather, and
to use lighter arms. Upon this the Welch were greatly alarmed, and submitted."

of the old Saxon shield. The shield of the Tapestry is of large size, and of the shape of a kite. It is in every instance flat. Here again we have another opportunity of judging of the minute accuracy of the Tapestry. Towards the end of the eleventh century the shield of a French knight is described [a] as having its surface not flat but convex, so as to embrace the person of the wearer. Other changes were speedily introduced; towards the close of the twelfth century it became shorter, and the bow at the top was flattened into a straight line. Thus it formed the " heater shield" of the middle ages.

The Norman shield when in use was carried by the arm, not the fist alone; two loops were placed on the inner side of it for the reception of the arm; when not wanted it was slung from the neck of the warrior; this is seen in several instances in the Tapestry. Many of the shields were ornamented with studs of metal, which were kept bright, so as to dazzle the sight of an antagonist. Others bear badges or devices, by which the bearer might be distinguished in the field.

From the earliest days, devices, answering the purpose of coats of arms, have been adopted. The tribes of Israel had their insignia. The armorial bearings of several Grecian chiefs are minutely described by the poets. The Roman legions had their characteristic symbols.[b] It was probably with this view that the

[a] Archæologia, vol. xxiv., p. 270.

[b] *See* Fenwick's Introduction to the *Slogans of the North of England,* and the Notes to the Introduction.

shields in the Tapestry were painted in the way in which we see them. A dragon is a common device; so also is a cross, the four arms of which proceed from the central stud in a sigmoidal curve.

Besides the insignia on the shields, ensigns and banners guided the movements of the armies and their various detachments.[a] The banner of the Norman army is invariably *argent, a cross or* in a *bordure azure*. This is repeated over and over again. We meet with it in the war against Conan, as well as at Pevensey and Hastings. There is no trace of the leopards or lions which shortly afterwards made their appearance in the arms of Normandy.

The different chieftains assembling under the Norman standard had each his pennon, gonfanon, or banner. None of these subsidiary standards are square, as the banner of a baron always was when the feudal system was developed. All the flags in the Tapestry have streamers attached to them, like those of a knight's pennon. It is not impossible, however, that these may represent the ribbons given to the Norman lords, as keepsakes by their ladies. Wace, in describing the battle of Val-des-dunes, says of Raol Tesson, that " he stood on one side afar off, having six score knights and six in his troop—all with their lances raised, *and trimmed with silk tokens.*" It would thus appear that the practice was not unusual, even in ordinary wars; how much more proper and becoming in a hazardous undertaking like the present. We know that the Norman lords had great difficulty in getting the leave of their ladies

---

[a] " And all had their cognizances, so that each might know his fellow, and Norman might not strike Norman, nor Frenchman kill his countryman, by mistake."

Taylor's Wace, p. 172.

XVII. WEAPONS AND ARMOUR ARE TAKEN ABOARD THE NORMAN SHIPS.

XVIII. THE INVASION FLEET CROSSES THE ENGLISH CHANNEL.

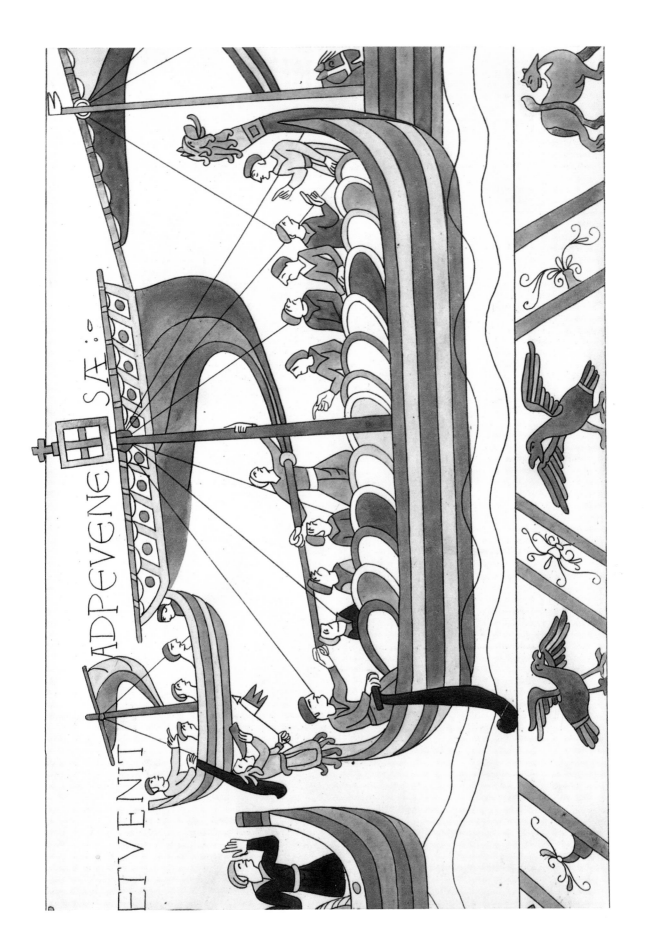

HIC·WILLELM·DVX·IN·MAGNO·NAVIGIO·MARE·TRANSIVIT·ET·VENIT·AD·PEVENE·SÆ:·

XIX. WILLIAM'S SHIPS APPROACH THE ENGLISH COAST AT PEVENSEY.

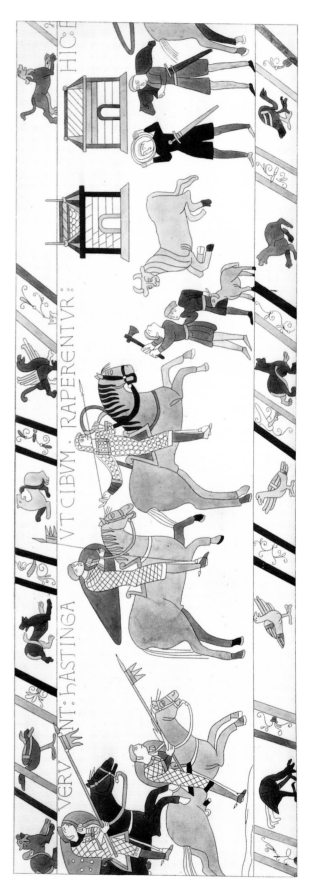

XX. THE NORMANS LAND AND BEGIN TO FORAGE AT HASTINGS.

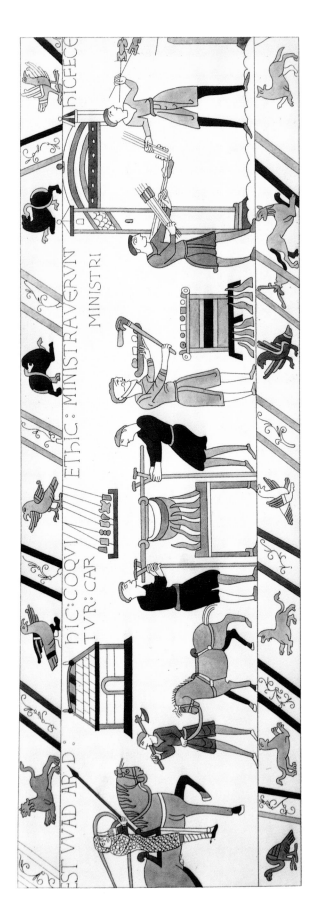

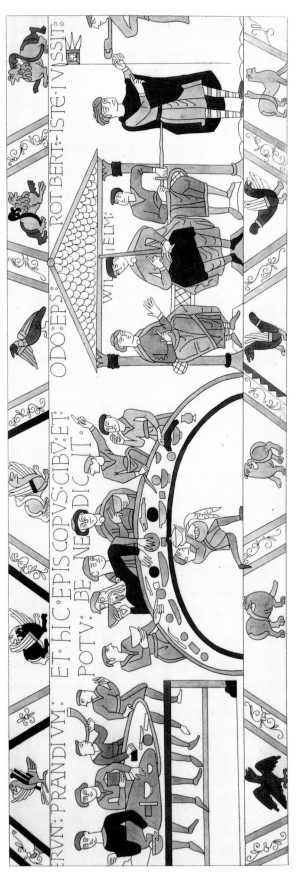

XXI. ON ENGLISH SOIL, THE NORMANS FEAST.

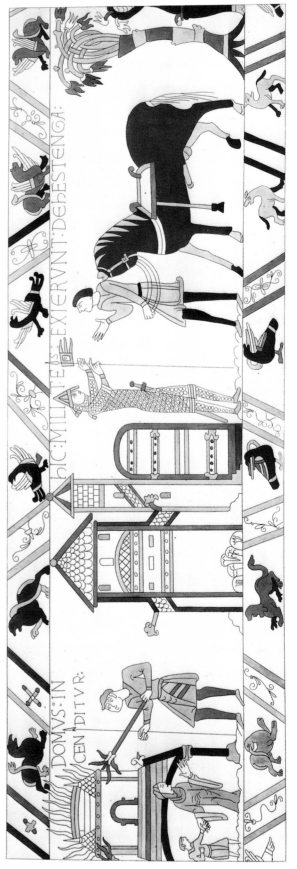

VT FONDERETVR CASTELLVM AT HESTENGA CEAST RA HIC NVNTIATVM EST WILLELM DE HAROLD HIC

HIC MILITES EXIERVNT DE HESTENGA

DOMVS IN CENDITVR

XXII. THE NORMANS ERECT FORTIFICATIONS WHILE LAYING WASTE THE AREA AND PREPARING FOR BATTLE.

HIC·NVNTIATVM·EST: WILLELM DE HAROLD

ENGA CEASTRA

XXIII. A SCOUT REPORTS THE MOVEMENTS OF THE ENGLISH ARMY.

XXIV. WILLIAM LEADS HIS SOLDIERS OUT TO BATTLE AND RECEIVES NEWS OF HAROLD.

to embark in the undertaking. Some feared the battle axes of the Saxon men, others dreaded the influence of the bright eyes of the Saxon ladies—a shrewd fear.[a]

Harold also had a standard. He planted it on the highest part of the eminence on which he marshalled his army for the fight, and by it he fought unflinchingly until cut down by the overpowering strength of the Norman chivalry. William of Malmesbury and several other writers tell us that Harold's standard was "in the form of a man fighting."[b] In the Tapestry it is a dragon. Wace does not describe it, but says, "His gonfanon was in truth a noble one, sparkling with gems and precious stones; after the victory William sent it to the Apostle to prove and commemorate his great conquest and glory."

A glance at the Tapestry will shew that the Saxons were entirely destitute of cavalry.[c] The comparatively limited size of the king-

[a] The Saxons as well as the Normans paid great attention to the opinions of the ladies, even upon martial subjects. Strutt says, they "would not go to battle or undertake any great expedition without consulting their wives, to whose advice they paid the greatest regard." This excellent antiquary pays more regard to truth than gallantry when in the same sentence he adds, "They also superstitiously placed great faith in the neighing of horses."—*Manners of the English*, vol i., p. 17.

[b] "This standard .. was sumptuously embroidered with gold and precious stones, in the form of a man fighting." Can Malmesbury have had in view here the description which Æschylus gives us of the shield of Polynices?

"His well-orb'd shield he holds,
New-wrought, and with double impress charged:
A warrior blazing all in golden arms,

Such their devices."

[c] Florence of Worcester distinctly states that it was "contrary to the custom of the English to fight on horseback."—*Bohn's Ed.* p. 157.

dom had rendered cavalry unnecessary for police purposes, and the Danes, the foreign enemies with whom the English had hitherto to contend, had too wide and stormy an ocean to cross, to attempt the transport of horses for the purposes of war. The great strength of the Norman army consisted in cavalry. William had been accustomed to contend with the King of France and other powerful chiefs in his immediate neighbourhood, and was thus compelled to avail himself of every device which human ingenuity had contrived for maintaining his cause.

The saddles of the horses are peculiar, having a high peak before and behind. We can readily understand how William, when he had become corpulent, received a mortal injury by coming down with violence upon the pommel of such a saddle. No horse armour is used, neither have any of the horses a saddle-cloth. " On the seal of Henry I. is the first representation of a saddle-cloth, and either during that reign or the preceding one, the high peak behind the saddle was altered for a back of greater breadth."[a] Most of the riders are provided with stirrups and with prick spurs. William's own horse was either an Arabian or a cross from an Arabian. It was presented to him by the King of Spain.

The Normans were strong in another force, of which the Saxons were almost entirely destitute—bowmen. In the Saxon lines there appears but one solitary bowman, whilst on the Norman side there are many. The Norman archers must have plied their shafts most diligently, for their arrows are sticking in the shields, and to some

[a] Meyrick, vol. i., p. 27.

extent in the bodies of the Saxons, like pins in a lady's pincushion. In the battle of Hastings the great event of the day turned upon an arrow skilfully sped. Had Harold's eye not been pierced, the battle would have been a drawn one, and in William's peculiar circumstance such a result was defeat.

The Saxon javelin differed from the Norman: it was short, and was used as a missile. In the Tapestry we see that some of the English have a bundle of spears in their hands, and that others are in the act of throwing them at the enemy. The Norman spear was a long one, adapted for use on horseback, and was employed in giving a thrust; one only therefore was required by each horseman. The Saxons darted their javelins at an approaching foe, and, when they came to close quarters, relied chiefly upon the vigorous use of the dreadful battle axe. As however at the battle of Hastings the Normans were on horseback, and were armed with long spears, it was with no small difficulty that the English could get within battle axe reach of their foes. In this way many of the Saxons were picked off before they could strike a blow. In Wace we have many examples of this—thus, he speaks of the knight of Tregoz, who "killed two Englishmen; smiting the one through with his lance, and braining the other with his sword; and then galloped his horse back, so that no Englishman touched him." In the Tapestry *(Plate XXVIII)* we see a horseman thrusting Leofwin, the brother of Harold, through with his lance, who in vain whirls his battle axe around him.

The battle axe of the Saxons had one disadvantage. "A man,"

P

says Wace, "when he wanted to strike with one of their hatchets, was obliged to hold it with both his hands, and could not at the same time, as it seems to me, both cover himself and strike with any freedom." This fact will account for the disastrous consequences of the retreat of the English at the battle of Hastings, after having been lured by the Normans into a pursuit.

The statements of Agathias, a writer of the sixth century, throw some light upon the Saxon mode of fighting. Speaking of the Franks (a kindred race), he says, "The arms of the Franks are very simple: they wear neither coat of mail nor greaves, but their legs and thighs are defended by bands of linen or leather. Their cavalry is inconsiderable, but they are formidable on foot; they wear a sword on the left thigh and carry a buckler. They use neither bow nor sling, but they are armed with double axes and *angones* [spears] with which they do most execution. These *angones* are of a length that may be both used as a javelin or in close fight against a charge of the enemy. The staff of this weapon is covered with iron laminæ or hoops, so that but very little wood appears, even down to the spike at the butt-end. On either side of the head of this javelin are certain barbs projecting downward close together as far as the shaft. The Frank soldier, when engaged with the enemy, casts his *angon*, which, if it enter the body, cannot be withdrawn in consequence of the barbs. Nor can the weapon be disengaged if it pierce the shield, for the bearer of the shield cannot cut it off because of the iron plates with which the staff is defended, while the Frank rushing forward jumps upon it as it trails on the ground, and thus bearing down his antagonist's defence, cleaves his skull with his axe, or transfixes him with a second javelin." [a]

In the Bayeux Tapestry the javelins in the hands of the Saxons are chiefly barbed, whilst the most of those in the hands of the Normans are lance-shaped, and are formed after the Roman model.

In *Cædmon's Paraphrase* and other Saxon illustrations the spears of the warriors are generally barbed. To what extent the hosts of Harold were armed with the true *angon*, the chief characteristic of which was a long iron shank, does not of course appear from the Tapestry, the scale being too small to allow of its minute delineation. The following cut exhibits the head of an *angon*, found in the well of the Roman station of Carvoran in Northumberland.

The sword of the combatants is chiefly remarkable for its great size. The Tapestry in this, as in other particulars, is strictly accurate. Mr. Akerman, after stating that several swords of large size had been found in Frank and Anglo-Saxon graves, says, "One of the finest examples which has ever come under my notice is that found at Fairford, in Gloucestershire, and recently exhibited by Mr. Wylie of that town. Its length, including the handle, is just three feet, the blade broad, two-edged, and pointed."

The only weapon that remains to be noticed is the mace or club.

[a] Akerman, in the Archæologia, vol. xxxiv.

This was a comparatively rude weapon, which ceased to be used as an instrument of offence after this period. At the battle of Hastings it seems to have been employed by the Saxons only. One is seen in the Tapestry *(Plate XXVI.)*, which has been thrown against the advancing line of the Normans, and at the close of the picture the retreating Saxons are seen to be armed with this weapon only.

From the review that we have taken of the equipment of the two armies, it is apparent that the English laboured under very great disadvantages. They were destitute of cavalry, with which the Normans were well provided; they had few archers, and they had no weapon that was a match for the long lance of the Normans. Strong in their insular position, they had neglected to adopt those improvements in the art of war which had been long adopted on the continent. We cannot wonder that, in despite of their native courage and astonishing personal prowess, the Saxons were overborne by the hosts of William on the field of Hastings.

It is time now to attend to the movements of the contending parties, and to trace them in their progress to the field on which their destiny was to be decided.

VII. THE LANDING.

"Et jam Argiva phalanx instructis navibus ibat."
Æn. II., 254.

THE vigorous manner in which William entered upon the preparations for his grand campaign excited the enthusiasm of his
continental neighbours. "Reports," says Ordericus Vitalis, "of
the expedition drew many valiant men from the adjoining
countries, who prepared their arms for battle. Thus the French
and Bretons, the Poitevins and Burgundians, and other people on
this side the Alps, flocked together for the war over the sea, and
scenting the booty which the conquest of Britain offered, were
prepared to undergo the various perils and chances, both by sea
and land, attending the enterprise." In the month of August
William's fleet assembled at the mouth of the river Dive,[a] in
the vicinity of which it is probable most of his ships were built.
Unfavourable weather detained it here for some time, and when it
did move, it was not able to proceed further than St. Valery-sur-
Somme. Adverse winds again prevailed for a month. "At this, says
Wace, "the barons were greatly wearied. Then they prayed the
Convent to bring out the shrine of St. Valery, and set it on a car-

[a] A stream which enters the sea a few miles to the east of the river Orne, upon
which the city of Caen is situated.

pet on the plain; and all came praying the holy relics that they might be allowed to pass over the sea. They offered so much money, that the relics were buried beneath it; and from that day forth they had good weather and a fair wind."

The long detention of the Norman forces on the French coast was a fortunate circumstance for them. Harold had made ample provision for resisting the landing of his opponent. With a fleet which he had assembled at Harwich he sailed to the Isle of Wight, and there throughout the summer and autumn months awaited William's arrival. He also kept a land force in suitable positions near the sea shore.[a] The same wind however which detained William at St. Valery brought Harold another foe which compelled him to withdraw his troops from the southern coast. On his departure the fleet was dispersed. Some of the chroniclers tell us that the seamen's time of service had expired, others that they were short of provisions. Harold's absence no doubt materially contributed to the demoralization of this important national safeguard.

Here we are again called upon to notice the vanity of man's policy. Harold foreseeing that a struggle would ensue between William and himself, and being, consequently, desirous of promoting friendly alliances with some of the continental powers, encouraged his brother Tostig to marry a daughter of the Earl of Flanders. This Tostig did, and thereby became brother-in-law to William of Normandy. Tostig, during the life of the Confessor,

[a] Roger de Hoveden, vol. i., 134. Ordericus Vitalis, vol. i., p. 464.

was appointed to the earldom of Northumbria, but the people having risen in arms against him, probably on account of the harshness
of his rule, he was removed, and Morcar appointed in his place.
When Harold became king, Tostig expected to be reinstated, but
so far from taking active measures in his favour, Harold married
the sister of the earl who had supplanted him. Tostig, enraged at
this treatment, conceived a violent hatred against his brother, and
inflamed the minds of the Earl of Flanders and the Duke of Normandy against him. Receiving, moreover, the active support of
Harold Hardrada, King of Norway, he landed with a hostile force
in Yorkshire, and ravaged the country. Harold, while watching the
proceedings of the Norman armada, heard of his brother's attempt.
Hastening northwards, he came upon him unawares, and slew both
him and Hardrada, and scattered their forces. While Harold was
engaged in these operations, William landed unopposed in Sussex!

It was on the night of the 29th September that the Norman expedition crossed the sea, and early next morning it
reached the port of Pavensey. The Tapestry represents this important transaction. The Duke's own ship is distinguished by the
consecrated banner at its mast head. This vessel was called the
Mora, and is stated to have been a present from the Duchess
Matilda. The legend in this part of the Tapestry *(Plate XIX)* is,
HIC WELELM: DUX IN MAGNO NAVIGIO MARE TRANSIVIT ET VENIT AD
PEVENSÆ[a]—Here Duke William in a large ship crossed the sea, and
arrived at Pevensey.

[a] Perhaps this is an elipsis for *ad litus Pevensæ;* more probably, however, these
irregularities of construction are to be ascribed to the low state of Latinity at the period.

A glance at the map of Sussex will shew that Pevensey was a most fitting place at which to effect a landing. Beachy Head projecting considerably to the south, protects this ancient port from the swell occasioned by the wind which most violently affects the English Channel—the south-west. The beach, too, is of a nature well adapted for allowing ships such as William's were being safely drawn up upon it. This was the port selected by the Conqueror for his embarkation when he returned to Normandy after his coronation. In all probability William's fleet would line the shore for a considerable space on both sides of Pevensey in the manner which they are represented as doing in the Tapestry, *(Plate XX)* It is curious to observe, that the remains of a vessel, which Mr. Lower thinks is at least as old as the Conquest, has recently been discovered, imbedded in the gravel of the ancient beach of Pevensey. The nature of the position in which it is placed prevents its being excavated; we might otherwise, perchance, have the pleasure of looking upon one of the Conqueror's own ships.

William landed with great caution. Wace thus describes the operation—" They arrived near Hastings, and there each ship was ranged by the other's side. There you might see the good sailors, the sergeants, and squires, sally forth and unload the ships; cast the anchors, haul the ropes, bear out shields and saddles, and land the war-horses and palfreys. The archers came forth, and touched land the foremost; each with his bow bent, and his quiver full of arrows slung at his side. All were shaven and shorn, and all clad in short garments, ready to attack, to shoot, to wheel about, and skirmish. All stood well equipped, and of good courage for the fight; and they scoured the whole shore, but found not an armed man there. After the archers had thus gone forth, the knights landed next, all armed, with their hauberks on, their shields slung at their necks, and their helmets laced They formed together on the shore, each armed upon his war-horse. All had their swords girded on, and passed into the plain with their lances raised."

Our picture-chronicle does not neglect these transactions. The inscription over them is, HIC EXEUNT CABALLI DE NAVIBUS ET HIC MILITES FESTINAVERUNT HASTINGA UT CIBUM RAPERENTUR[a]—Here the horses disembark, and here the soldiers hurry forward to Hastings to seize food.

An incident is told respecting the landing of William which is best related in the words of the Chronicler. " As the ships were drawn to shore, and the Duke first landed, he fell by chance upon his two hands. Forthwith all raised a loud cry of distress, 'an evil sign' said they, 'is here.' But he cried out lustily, 'See seigniors, by the splendour of God! I have seized England with my two hands; without challenge no prize can be made; all is our own that is here; now we shall see who will be the bolder man.' Then one of his men ran forward and put his hand on a hut, and took a handful of the thatch and turned to the Duke, saying heartily, 'Sire, come forward and receive seizin; of this land I give you seizin;

A stroke has probably been over the last A in *Hastinga*, so as to make it *Hastingam*, which the construction requires. *Raperentur* seems to have been used as a deponent verb, contrary to classical usage.

without doubt the country is yours.' And the Duke said, 'I ac-
cept it; may God be with us.' " [a]

The nature of the ground prevented William from proceeding
directly up the country from Pevensey. So late as the days of
Queen Elizabeth, the land inwards from this point was little better
than a marsh. The Ordnance map of Sussex shows, in this direction, a remarkable absence of towns and villages, indicating pretty
clearly what it must have been in former times. William went
cautiously along the shore to Hastings, where he erected his fortifications, and refreshed his troops. In the Tapestry we see them
seizing the sheep and cattle in the fields, cooking their food, and
afterwards seating themselves at table. Wace says "Before
evening had set in they had finished a fort. Then you might see
them make their kitchens, light their fires, and cook their meat.
The Duke sat down to eat, and the barons and knights had food in

---

[a] This was not the first occasion on which a similar occurrence took place.
The following passage bearing upon the subject may interest the reader:—
"Thou sayest well Sancho (quoth Don Quixote), but I must tell thee that times are
wont to vary and change their course; and what are commonly accounted omens by
the vulgar, though not within the scope of reason, the wise will nevertheless regard
as incidents of lucky aspect. Your watcher of omens rises betimes, and going
abroad, meets a Franciscan friar, whereupon he hurries back again, as if a furious
dragon had crossed his way. Another happens to spill the salt upon the table, and
straightway his soul is overcast with the dread of coming evil: as if nature had
willed that such trivial accidents should give notice of ensuing mischances, The
wise man and good christian will not, however, pry too curiously into the counsels
of heaven. Scipio, on arriving in Africa, stumbled as he leapt on shore; his soldiers took it for an ill omen, but he, embracing the ground, said, 'Africa, thou
canst not escape me—I have thee fast.' "—*Don Quixote*, Part II. chap. lviii.

plenty; for they had brought ample store. All ate and drank enough, and were right glad that they were ashore."

The culinary operations of the invading force require some notice. Although some huts have been erected on the shore, having been brought in frame with the fleet, the cooks discharge their duties in the open air.

> ". . . . . . A kettle slung
> Between two poles upon a stick transverse
> Receives the morsel . . . . ."

The pot may have been a metallic vessel brought over from Normandy with the stores; its appearance, however, strongly reminds us of a plan which Froissart tells us the Scotch adopted in one of their incursions into England. Having seized an ox, they slaughtered it, and boiled its flesh in its skin, supporting the extemporaneously-made cauldron after the manner shown in the Tapestry. The rest of the cookery is done upon a hearth. A spit, on which the wood is placed, is thrust into the ground, so as to suspend the article to be cooked a short way above the fire. At the present day much of the cookery of Normandy is done by placing the food in earthenware vessels, which are brought into contact with the embers without the intervention of a grate. The food when cooked was usually, at this period, handed to the guests seated at the table, on the spits, who took it off with their fingers, assisted with a knife which they carried with them. Forks were comparatively unknown for some centuries after the Conquest.

In the Tapestry two tables are spread. The first of them seems to be formed of shields set upon a frame. The persons seated at it are probably some of William's chief officers whose duty it is to arrange the entertainment, and taste the food and wine previous to its being set before the Duke. William sits at a table which was no doubt brought from Normandy. It is of classic form, being like that called by the Romans Sigma, from its resemblance to the Greek letter of that name, which in the time of the Roman Emperors was formed like our C. The guests sit at one side of it only, the inner or concave side being left open, to allow the servants more readily to approach. All the operations of the table are presented to us by the artist. Odo, with his thumb and two forefingers extended, is blessing the food and the drink. William has planted his hand upon the principal dish, as if to claim the lion's share for himself. Another person is tearing a fish to pieces with his fingers, and conveying the morsels by the same medium to his mouth. An old man with a beard, probably William's Nestor, who refused to comply with the tonsured fashion of the day, is drinking with his neighbour; both of them have uplifted bowls. A servant upon bended knee is presenting a covered dish to the party. These compartments are respectively described, HIC COQUITUR CARO ET HIC MINISTRAVERUNT MINISTRI— Here the food is being cooked and here the attendants have served up the viands: HIC FECERUNT PRANDIUM ET HIC EPISCOPUS CIBUM ET POTUM BENEDICIT—Here they have prepared the feast and here the bishop is blessing the meat and drink.

The meal must necessarily have been a hasty one. One of the guests has already risen from his seat, and calls the attention of the Duke to something that is passing without.

William was now fairly committed to a great and hazardous undertaking, and retreat was not to be thought of; at the same time, the utmost circumspection was necessary, and the Duke of Normandy was not the man to neglect any precaution.

We accordingly next find him in solemn consultation with his two uterine brothers—Odo, Archbishop of Bayeux, and Robert, Count of Mortaine. William has his sword elevated, and Robert is in the act of drawing his from the scabbard—indications which strongly mark the nature of the attempt before them. The legend over this group *(Plate XXI)* is simply, ODO EPISCOPUS: ROBERTUS —Odo the Bishop: Robert.

As the result, probably, of the deliberations of the three brothers, it was resolved strongly to fortify the position occupied by William's army. Such was the importance of this work, that William, with the consecrated banner in his hand, is seen personally superintending it. The spades of the workmen are worthy of observation. They are evidently made of wood, but shod with iron. They have a notch for the foot on one side only. That they were adapted not merely for turning up the soil, but for trenching the scull of an enemy, is evident not only from their size and form, but from the use to which they are put by two of the parties before us. The inscription over this part is, ISTE JUSSIT UT FODERETUR CASTELLUM AT HESTENGA[M]—He has ordered an intrenchment to be

dug at Hastings; and over the castle itself is written, CEASTRA[a]—
The camp.

The camp in question could not be the castle, the ruins of which
now crown the heights of Hastings. However strong the position of
Hastings castle, there is not space enough on the rocky platform on
which it stands for the encampment of an army one fourth of the
size of William's; besides, we cannot suppose that William in his
present circumstances would attempt the erection of a fort of solid
masonry. The camp which William constructed was, as the Tapestry leads us to believe, formed of earth, strengthened with wooden
palisades, the whole being commanded at intervals by towers
which had been brought in frame from France. The phrase *ut
foderetur*, that they might *dig* a castle, is express, and the men are
seen throwing up the soil. This agrees with what Wace says,
" They enclosed a fort and strengthened it round about with palisades and a fosse." Some extensive entrenchments, still to be seen
in the immediate vicinity of the railway station at Hastings, are
probably the remains of the Duke's encampment. [b]

An English knight, who had watched the landing of William,

---

[a] It has been argued from the occurrence of AT instead of AD, and of CEASTRA for
CASTRA, in these inscriptions, that the clerk who wrote them was an Englishman.
It must, however, be borne in mind that the original Norman language, which had
a common origin with the Saxon, was at the period of the Conquest spoken in com-
parative purity at Bayeux. In other parts of the duchy French prevailed.

[b] It was my privilege when wandering over the ground rendered memorable by
the battle of Hastings to enjoy the companionship of Mr. Lower, of Lewes. To his
local knowledge, his extensive acquaintance with antiquarian science, and his
friendly attention, I am largely indebted.

hastened to Harold with the alarming news. He found him re-joicing after the defeat of Tostig and Hardrada. "Foolish" says Wace, "is he who glorifies himself, for good fortune soon passeth away. The heart of man often rejoiceth when ruin is nigh."

Bitterly did Harold grieve that he had not been at the spot when the Normans landed, that he might have driven them into the sea. "It is a sad mischance," said he, "but thus it hath pleased our Heavenly King."

Harold had, by the rapidity of his marches, surprised his brother Tostig, and come upon the troops of Hardrada unawares. He thought to adopt the same policy with William; and, without taking time to refresh or recruit his exhausted army, commenced his march southwards. In the course of a few days he was in the vicinity of his enemy. William, however, was not to be taken by surprise, and Harold was constrained to take up a position at Battle, distant about six miles from Hastings, where the Duke was encamped.

The next compartment in the Tapestry exhibits to us William giving audience to a messenger who announces to him the approach of Harold. The legend is, HIC NUNTIATUM EST WILLELMO DE HAROLD —Here news is brought to William respecting Harold.

Whilst these movements were going on, the inhabitants of the southern shore of Sussex were suffering severely. Not only were their cattle taken from the folds, and their recently replenished granaries emptied, but their dwellings were wantonly destroyed. Perhaps the Saxons may have provoked the vengeance of the foe, for they were not men to take quietly the spoiling of their goods.

In the Tapestry we see a soldier setting fire to a house (one being the representative of many), from which a female and child are escaping—escaping from present destruction to be cast, with winter before them, houseless, friendless, and without food, upon the wide world. The sufferings of the battle field form but a small part of the horrors of war. This compartment of the work bears the inscription, HIC DOMUS INCENDITUR—Here a house is set fire to. Some outlined figures in the margin of this part of the work doubtless refer to those distressing immoralities which too often attend the march of armies.

Whilst the two armies lay within a few miles of each other several messages passed between the commanders. William was too good a soldier to risk a battle if he could avoid it. He therefore sent a tonsured monk to Harold, reminding him of his oath, and calling upon him to deliver up the kingdom. Harold, flushed with recent victory, was with difficulty restrained from cutting down the messenger; as it was, he sent him away with insults. When his rage had subsided he saw his folly, and sent an envoy, acquainted with the language of France, to duke William, offering to make him a pecuniary recompense if he would recross the sea, telling him however, if he did not, he would give him battle on the following Saturday.

Saturday, the 1st of October, was Harold's birth day. He always regarded it as his fortunate day; and he was anxious if he did enter into mortal conflict with a desperate foe, that it should be when his propitious star was in the ascendant. Like another of

England's heroes—Oliver Cromwell—the day of his birth was to prove the day of his death.

A battle now being imminent, Gurth, the brother of Harold, was exceedingly anxious that the king should retire from the host and give the command to him. Gurth had taken no oath to William, and therefore had not the punishment of perjury to fear. Besides, if he were slain, England would still have her king; and army after army could be raised, if need be, to resist the pretensions of any invader. Harold refused to adopt the wise counsel of his brother. Though a brave man, he had not the self-command of William, nor the same power of taking an enlarged view of a subject.

The day before the battle, Harold and Gurth rode out early in the morning to descry the enemy. " They rode on, viewing and examining the ground, till, from a hill where they stood, they could see the Norman host, who were near. They saw a great many huts made of branches of trees, tents well equipped, pavilions, and gonfanons; and they heard horses neighing, and beheld the glittering of armour. They stood a long while without speaking " —and at length returned in silence to their tent. They had seen enough to awaken their apprehensions, and to make them anxious for further information. Harold, therefore, sent out two spies to reconnoitre. They fell into the hands of the Normans, who brought them to William. He used them well, and ordered them to be conducted through the host. On their return they reported that the Normans, whom they had noticed to be close shaven and cropt, were an army of priests and mass-sayers rather than

R

knights. Harold, who knew the habits of the Normans, replied, "These are valiant knights, bold and brave warriors, though they bear not beards and mustaches as we do."

Notwithstanding the ill success of his former representations, William persevered in negotiation. He lost no time by it, and if he did not succeed in his immediate object, he induced his observers to believe, that one who was so bent upon the investigation of his claims must have right upon his side.

On the same day that he entertained the spies of Harold, he sent a monk, learned and wise, offering Harold one of three things— that he should resign the kingdom, that he should submit to the judgment of the Pope, or meet him singly and fight body for body. Harold declined every alternative.

Next day—the day before the battle—William attempted to obtain a personal interview with Harold. Harold refused to meet him. By the messenger who brought Harold's negative to the proposal for a meeting, William sent him word that if he would retire he would give him all Northumberland, and whatever belonged to the kingdom beyond the Humber; to his brother Gurth he promised the lands of Godwin their father. Harold rejected this also: Northumberland was nothing worth; it was chiefly peopled by Danes, and was liable to constant invasion. William, when king, could not govern Northumberland. As a matter, not of feeling, not of revenge, but of cool, calculating state policy, he swept it of every living thing—he made it a desert, and such it continued for a century after his time.

At the same time that William sent his last message, he charged the clerk who took it, in case of refusal, to sow the seeds of terror and dissatisfaction among the English. "Tell them," said he, "that all who come with Harold, or support him in this affair, are excommunicated by the Apostle and his clergy." This was a javelin skilfully thrown. "At this excommunication the English were much troubled; they feared it greatly, and the battle still more."

Gurth, however, rallied them. He told them that their all was at stake, that William had promised their lands to his followers, and that he had already taken homage for them from many. "Defend yourselves then," he said, "and your children and all that belongs to you, while you may."

At these words the English were aroused, and cried out that the Normans had come on an evil day, and had embarked on a foolish matter.

"The Duke and his men tried no further negotiation, but returned to their tents, sure of fighting on the morrow. Then men were to be seen on every side straightening lances, fitting hauberks and helmets, making ready the saddles and stirrups; filling the quivers, stringing the bows, and making all ready for the battle."

The night before a battle must be a season of peculiar solemnity and suspense. The shades of night, giving indistinctness to the landscape, harmonize too well with the doubts which becloud the mind as to the morrow's destiny. He is a fool, not a hero, who would step from time into eternity without solemn thought.

The accounts which we have of the way in which the hosts spent the night before the battle are all to the disadvantage of the English. Had they been the winning instead of the losing party, the chroniclers would doubtless have been less severe. As it is, they tell us that the troops of Harold spent the night in eating and drinking and merriment—never lying down in their beds. If this be true, how we are we to account for the vigour with which they fought from nine o'clock in the morning until nightfall next day? The Normans and French, on the other hand, we are told, betook themselves to their orisons. "They made confession of their sins, accused themselves to the priests, and vowed that they would never more eat flesh on the Saturday" (the day of the battle). Many of them kept the vow!

At the dawn of day each party had completed its preparations. Before the sun should set, a battle was to be fought on which hung not merely the fate of an empire, but, as events have subsequently proved, the destinies of the civilized world to this hour.

THE BATTLE.

"Revolving in his altered soul
The various turns of fate below."
Dryden.

THE room is still pointed out in the roofless donjon keep of Falaise, in which Arlotte, the tanner's daughter, gave birth to William the Conqueror. It is a small comfortless apartment. When the new-born babe was laid upon the floor, he grasped the straw which covered it with a vigour that induced the bystanders to predict that he would ere long take a foremost place amongst the ambitious potentates of his age. In the course of our worsted narrative we have followed our hero to a point in which he is about to justify the correctness of these surmisings.

Harold, painfully conscious of the inferiority of his military equipments, resolved to act on the defensive. He took up his position on a round-topped hill, having on its summit a circular platform just sufficient to contain his troops drawn up in close order. This hill was anciently called Senlac; it afterwards became the site of the Abbey of Battle. Harold further strengthened his position by earthen ramparts crowned with palisades of wood. Wace, speaking of these precautions, says, "They had built up a fence before them with their shields, and with ash and other wood; and had well joined and wattled in their whole work, so as not to leave even a crevice; and thus they had a barricade in their front, through which any Norman who would attack them must first pass. Being covered in this way by their shields and barricades, their aim was to defend themselves; and if they had remained steady for that purpose, they would not have been conquered that day; for every Norman who made his way in lost his life in dishonour, either by hatchet or bill, by club or other weapon." In addition to these defences, Wace tells us that Harold "made a fosse, which went across the field, guarding one side of their army." This was probably lower down the hill than the position occupied by his camp, and was chiefly intended to incommode the cavalry.

Harold further feeling that he had not the power to prevent the enemy's horse outflanking him, ordered " that all should be ranged with their faces towards the enemy"—that they should front three sides at least of the square. We see them (*Plate XXVIII*) sustaining an attack from opposite quarters, and in both cases fronting the foe. He moreover issued directions " that no one should move from where he was; so that whoever came might find them ready; and that whatever any one, be he Norman or other, should do, each should do his best to defend his own place." He planted his standard—the dragon of Wessex—on the most elevated part of the hill, and there he resolved to defend it to the last. Nobly Harold fulfilled his purpose—nothing could tempt him from his post—and ere the Saxon ensign bowed to the banner blessed by the Pope, his blood had drenched the soil.

Harold's men consisted but in part of regularly trained troops. Amongst them were many "villains called together from the villages, bearing such arms as they found—clubs and great picks, iron forks and stakes." These undisciplined Saxons exhibited no lack of that indomitable energy for which the English race is famous; but, as Harold's brother, Gurth, remarked, "a great gathering of vilanaille is worth little in battle."

The numbers of the two armies have been variously stated. Probably Wace is right in saying that they were nearly equal. He sets down the army of William at sixty thousand, and speaks thus of his opponent's: "Many and many have said that Harold had but a small force, and that he fell on that account. But many others say, and so do I, that he and the Duke had man for man. The men of the Duke were not more numerous, but he had certainly more barons, and the men were better. He had plenty of good knights, and great plenty of good archers."

The Norman forces, having finished their devotions by an early hour in the morning, were ordered to form in three divisions, the Duke himself commanding the centre, which consisted of Normans. William then addressed his army, saying, " If I conquer, you will conquer; if I win lands, you shall have lands"—telling them, at the same time, that he came not merely to establish his own claims, but also to punish the English for the massacre of the Danes, and other felonies which they had committed against his people. Then they began to cry out, " You will not see one coward; none here will fear to die for love of you if need be." And he answered them, "Strike hard at the beginning; stay not to take spoil; all the booty shall be in common, and there will be plenty for every one. There will be no safety in peace or flight. The English will neither love nor spare Normans. Felons they were, and are; false they were, and false they will be."

William was continuing his speech, when Fitz-Osborne, who had been one of his principal advisers in the whole business, interrupted him: "Sire, said he, we tarry here too long; let us arm ourselves. *Allons ! Allons !*"

When William began to prepare for battle, he called first for his good hauberk, and a man brought it on his arm and placed it before him; but, in putting his head in to get it on, he inadvertently turned it the wrong way, with the back in front. He quickly changed it; but when he saw that those who stood by him were sorely alarmed, he said, "I never believed in omens, and I never will. I trust in God. The hauberk which was turned wrong and then set right, signifies that I who have hitherto been but duke, shall be changed into a king. Then he crossed himself, and straightway took his hauberk, stooped his head, and put it on aright; and laced his helmet and girt his sword, which a varlet brought him."

There is something poetical in the error which William made. He was too good a general to be boastful—he had been too often in the field not to know the difference between the putting on and the putting off of the armour—he knew too well, moreover, the serious nature of the venture which he had made to pay much attention to the duties of his military toilet. His capacious mind was weighing the chances of victory or defeat, and for the last time reviewing all the arrangements which he had made for either alternative. The Norman Duke, notwithstanding his usual exemption from superstitious influences, did not consider his preparation for battle complete until he had strung around his neck a portion of the relics over which Harold had taken his faithless vow. William entrusted the standard which the Pope had given him to Turstin Fitz-Rou. His demeanour, rendered even more than usually commanding by the greatness of the occasion, seems to have attracted the attention of his companions in arms;—" Never (said the Viscount of Toarz), never have I seen a man so fairly armed, nor one who rode so gallantly, or bore his arms or became his hauberk so well; neither any one who bore his lance so gracefully, or sat his horse or manœuvred so nobly. There is no such knight under heaven! a fair knight he is, and a fair king he will be !"

We are now prepared for examining the Tapestry. Under the compartment inscribed HIC MILITES EXIERUNT DE HESTENGA—Here the soldiers have departed from Hastings—we see the Duke, armed cap-a-pie, preparing to mount his charger, which is brought him by an attendant. Next we have a well arranged group of horsemen, representing the whole Norman army, proceeding onward at a steady pace. Some scouts in advance scour the country, and guard against surprise. The inscription proceeds, ET VENERUNT AD PRELIUM CONTRA HAROLDUM REGEM—And march to battle against Harold the King.

The country between Hastings and Battle is of an undulating

S

nature. The Duke had many defiles of a dangerous nature to pass, in which Harold might have harassed him if he had possessed cavalry, and if he had had troops to spare. As it was, he was allowed to proceed unmolested; nevertheless, both parties sent out scouts to watch each other's movements. The horseman, Vitalis, seems to have been sent on this errand by William. In the Tapestry he is represented as galloping up to his chieftain with the news which he has gathered respecting the enemy, towards whom his spear is pointed. The group is labelled, HIC WILLELM: DUX INTERROGAT VITAL: SI VIDISSET EXERCITUM HAROLDI—Here Duke William asks Vitalis, whether he had seen Harold's army.

Harold's scout is next seen, on foot, endeavouring to obtain a glimpse through the forests of the approaching foe; he then informs his king of their advance. The legend is, ISTE NUNTIAT HAROLDUM REGEM DE EXERCITU WILLELM: DUCIS—This man brings word to Harold the King respecting Duke William's army. "The line of the Normans' march from the camp of Hastings to the battle-field, must have lain on the south-western slope of the elevated ridge of land extending from Fairlight to Battle; that is, to the north of the village of Hollington, through what is now Crowhurst Park, to the elevated spot called Hetheland, but now known as Telham Hill."[a] This hill is about a mile south of the one occupied by Harold. Its ancient name seems to imply that it was covered with heath rather than with wood; this circumstance, together with the fact of its elevated position, would enable Wil-

---

[a] Lower on the Battle of Hastings, 'Sussex Arch. Col.,' vi. 18.

liam's host for the first time clearly to descry their enemy from its summit, and render it a fitting place on which to make the final preparations for the onslaught. This spot, according to local tradition, derived its name of Telham, or Telman Hill, from William's having told off his men before advancing to the fight.

We can readily conceive what would be the feelings of the two forces, as on the morning of the 14th of October, 1066, they came in sight of each other;—"Some with their colour rising, others turning pale ; some making ready their arms, others raising their shields ; the brave man raising himself to the fight, the coward trembling at the approaching danger." Who can stand upon the ground occupied by either party without sympathizing, in part, with their fierce emotions ? Happily, such sympathy is vain. Not only have victor and vanquished long ceased to be moved by earth's concernments, but the descendants of each have long been blended into one race, having common interests, common feelings.

Before commencing the onslaught, William again addressed his troops. He is represented in the Tapestry *(Plate XXV.)* beside a tree, representing probably the edge of the forest, with the baton of command in his right hand. The legend here is, HIC WILLELM : DUX ALLOQUITUR SUIS MILITIBUS UT PREPARARENT SE VIRILITER ET SAPIENTER AD PRELIUM CONTRA ANGLORUM EXERCITUM—Here Duke William exhorts his soldiers to prepare manfully and prudently for battle against the army of the English. Wace says that the battle-cry of the Normans was *Dex aie !* (God help !), that of the English, *Ut !* (out !—begone !)

Harold was not less diligent than his antagonist in making preparations. " He ordered the men of Kent to go where the Normans were likely to make the attack ; for they say that the men of Kent are entitled to strike first, and that whenever the king goes to battle, the first blow belongs to them. The right of the men of London is to guard the king's body, to place themselves around him, and to guard his standard ; and they were accordingly placed by the standard to watch and defend it." " Each man had a hauberk on, with his sword girt, and his shield at his neck. Great hatchets were also slung at their necks, with which they expected to strike heavy blows. They were on foot in close ranks, and carried themselves right boldly. *Olicrosse* (holy cross) they often cried, and many times repeated *Godamite* (God Almighty)."[a] " And now behold ! that battle was gathered whereof the fame is yet mighty."

Nearly all the chroniclers tell us that the minstrel-warrior Taillefer was the first to begin the battle, and some of them inform us that as he approached the English lines, he produced a sort of panic amongst them by his juggling tricks. It says not a little for the correctness of the delineations of the Tapestry, and of the authenticity of the *Roman de Rou*, that neither of them refers to these improbable stories, however great the pictorial effect of them might have been. As, however, the verses of Gaimar, describing the

---

[a] During the middle ages the English were much given to the irreverent use of this great name ; so much so was this the case, that *Godamites* became, in France, synonymous with English. Joan of Arc usually designates her enemies by this term.

apocryphal exploits of Taillefer, possess considerable interest, it may be well to introduce them here in the garb in which they have been clothed by Mr. Amyot, in the *Archæologia*,[a]

" Foremost in the bands of France,
    Arm'd with hauberk and with lance,
    And helmet glittering in the air,
    As if a warrior-knight he were,
    Rushed forth the minstrel Taillefer.—
    Borne on his courser swift and strong,
        He gaily bounded o'er the plain,
    And raised the heart-inspiring song
    (Loud echoed by the warlike throng)
        Of Roland and of Charlemagne,
    Of Oliver, brave peer of old,
        Untaught to fly, unknown to yield,
    And many a knight and vassal bold,
    Whose hallowed blood, in crimson flood,
        Dyed Roncevalles' field.

    Harold's host he soon descried,
    Clustering on the hill's steep side :
    Then turned him back brave Taillefer,
    And thus to William urged his prayer :
    ' Great Sire, it fits not me to tell
    How long I've served you, or how well ;
    Yet if reward my lays may claim,
    Grant now the boon I dare to name :
    Minstrel no more, be mine the blow
    That first shall strike yon perjured foe.'
    ' Thy suit is gained,' the Duke replied,
    ' Our gallant minstrel be our guide.'
    ' Enough,' he cried, ' with joy I speed,
    Foremost to vanquish or to bleed.'

[a] Vol. xix., p. 206. Mr. Amyot does not profess to adhere strictly to the text of Gaimar, but has introduced into his translation some incidents mentioned by other writers.

And still of Roland's deeds he sung,
While Norman shouts responsive rung,
As high in air his lance he flung,
   With well directed might;
Back came the lance into his hand,
Like urchin's ball, or juggler's wand,
And twice again, at his command,
   Whirled it's unerring flight.—
While doubting whether skill or charm
Had thus inspired the minstrel's arm,
The Saxons saw the wondrous dart
Fixed in their standard-bearer's heart.

Now thrice aloft his sword he threw,
   'Midst sparkling sunbeams dancing,
And downward thrice the weapon flew,
Like meteor o'er the evening dew,
   From summer sky swift glancing :
And while amazement gasped for breath,
Another Saxon groaned in death.

More wonders yet!—on signal made,
   With mane erect, and eye-balls flashing,
The well-taught courser rears his head,
   His teeth in ravenous fury gnashing;
He snorts—he foams—and upward springs—
   Plunging he fastens on the foe,
And down his writhing victim flings,
   Crushed by the wily minstrel's blow.
Thus seems it to the hostile band
Enchantment all, and fairy land.

Fain would I leave the rest unsung :—
The Saxon ranks, to madness stung,
Headlong rushed with frenzied start,
Hurling javelin, mace, and dart;
No shelter from the iron shower
Sought Taillefer in that sad hour;

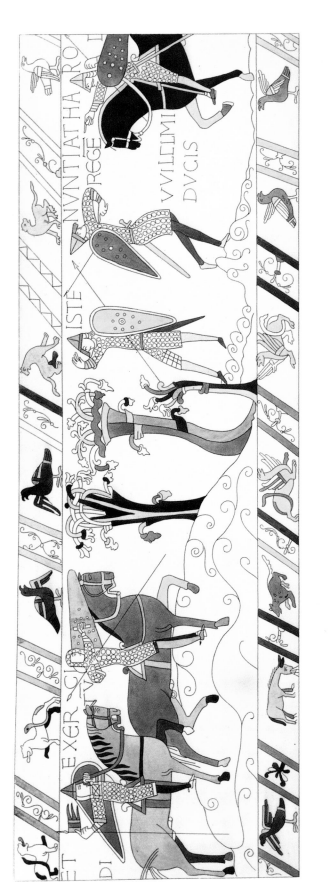

XXV. THE ARMIES DRAW NEAR; WILLIAM ADDRESSES HIS TROOPS.

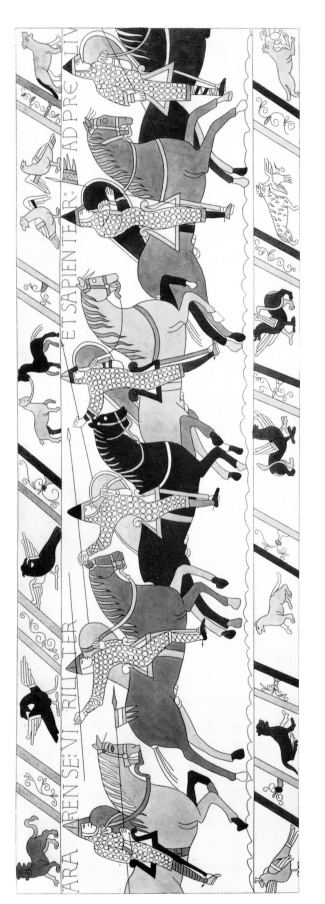

XXVI. THE BATTLE OF HASTINGS. THE NORMAN CAVALRY CHARGE FORTH.

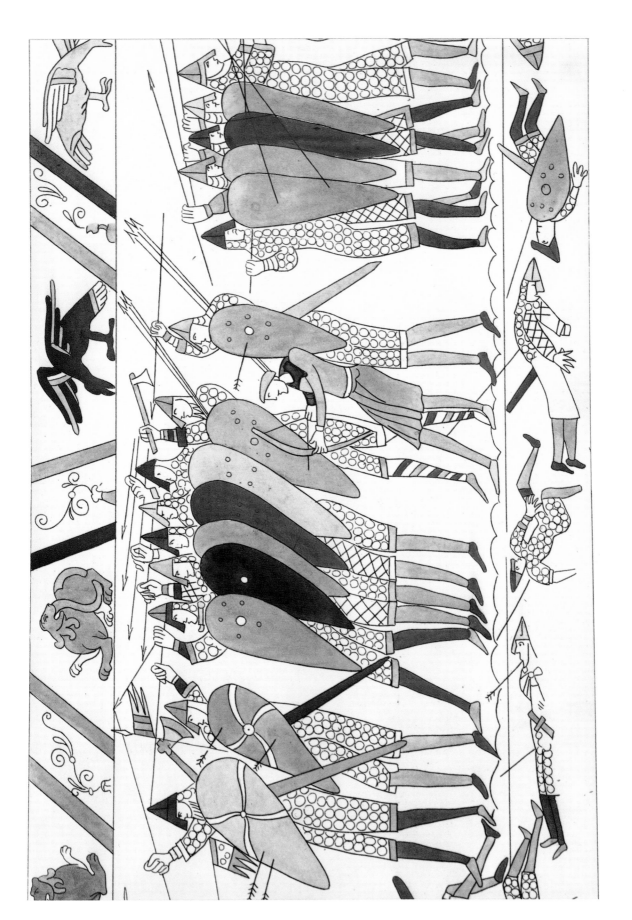

XXVII. THE ENGLISH ARMY, DRAWN UP IN CLOSE RANKS ON FOOT, RECEIVES THE NORMAN ATTACK.

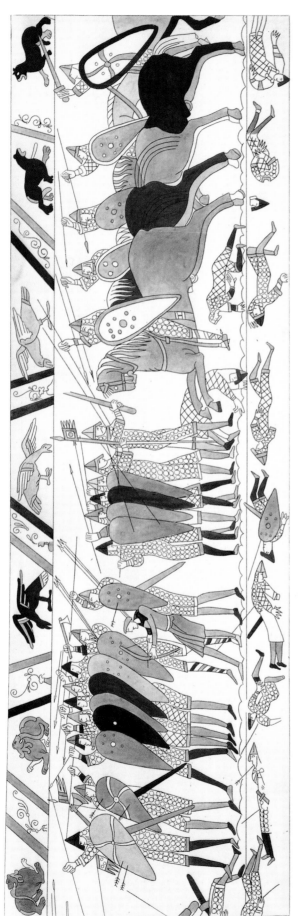

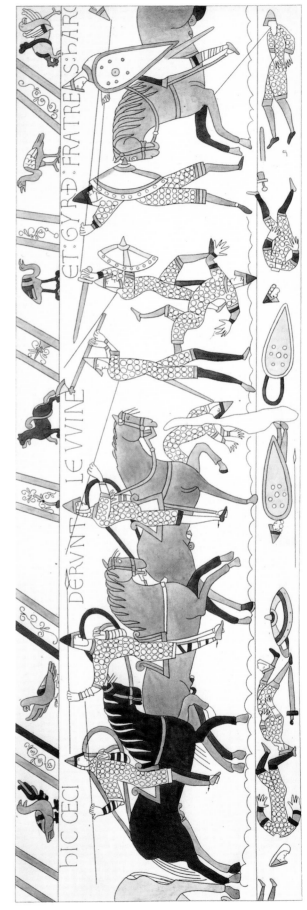

HIC CECI DERVNT LEVVINE ET GYRD FRATRES HAROL

XXVIII. HAROLD'S BROTHERS LEOFWIN AND GURTH ARE SLAIN.

XXIX. THE BATTLE RAGES. THE NORMANS ATTACK THE ENGLISH HILLTOP POSITION; THEN ODO RALLIES THEM.

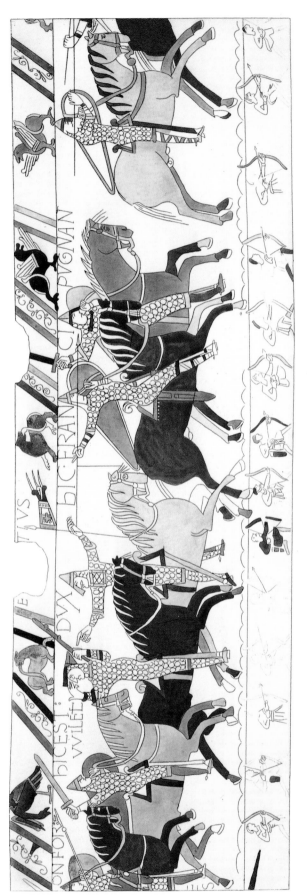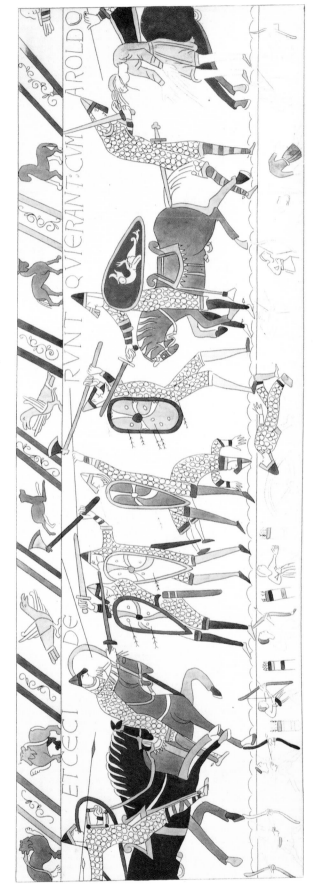

XXX. DUKE WILLIAM REFUTES THE RUMOUR OF HIS DEATH AND ENCOURAGES HIS MEN, WHO BEGIN TO INFLICT GRIEVOUS LOSSES ON HAROLD'S ARMY.

XXXI. THE DEATH OF KING HAROLD.

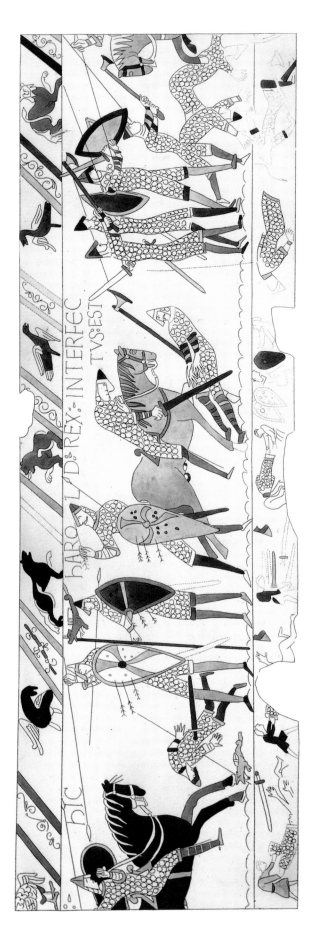

XXVII. HAROLD IS SLAIN: THE ENGLISH FLEE THE FIELD.

> Yet still he beckoned to the field,
> ' Frenchmen, come on—the Saxons yield—
> Strike quick—strike home—in Roland's name—
> For William's glory—Harold's shame.'
> Then pierced with wounds, stretched side by side,
> The minstrel and his courser died."

The charge of Taillefer roused the mettle of both parties. " Forthwith arose the noise and cry of war, and on either side the people put themselves in motion." " Some were striking, others urging onwards ; and all were bold, and cast aside fear "

" Loud and far resounded the bray of the horns and the shocks of the lances ; the mighty strokes of clubs, and the quick clashing of swords. One while the Englishmen rushed on, another while they fell back ; one while the men from over the sea charged onwards, and again, at other times, retreated. Then came the cunning manœuvres, the rude shocks and strokes of the lance, and blows of the sword, among the sergeants and soldiers, both English and Norman. When the English fall the Normans shout. Each side taunts and defies the other, yet neither knoweth what the other saith ; and the Normans say the English bark, because they understand not their speech." In this way the struggle proceeded for several hours. The Saxons had an arduous part to sustain ; for, as shewn in the Tapestry, they were attacked on all sides.

Early in the battle the brothers of Harold, Gurth and Leofwin, fell. The fact is indicated by the superscription, HIC CECIDERUNT LEWINE ET GURTH FRATRES HAROLDI REGIS—Here fell Leofwin and Gurth, the brothers of Harold the King. Bravely had they sustained their brother in his efforts to resist the invader, and doubt-less they had, in the excess of their zeal, needlessly hazarded their lives. According to Wace, they did not fall until after Harold had been slain. This is one of the points in which the worsted chronicle differs from the *Roman de Rou.* In a battle, where all is confusion—where few can obtain a general view of what passes—and where each is intensely occupied with his own foeman—it is exceedingly difficult for any one to give a just account of the whole scene, or to reconcile the conflicting statements of others. All our historians agree that both the brothers of Harold were slain in the battle of Hastings ;—had it been otherwise William would not have been crowned at Westminister that Christmas.

Following, on the Tapestry, the death of Gurth and Leofwin *(Plate XXIX)* is a scene thus labelled : HIC CECIDERUNT SIMUL ANGLI ET FRANCI IN PRELIO. The scene is here most animated. Saxons and Normans are mingled in a close encounter. Horses and men exhibit the frantic contortions of dying agony. At the further end of the compartment a party of Saxons, posted on a hill, exposed to the enemy on one side, but protected by a forest (represented by a tree) on the other, seem to be making head against their assailants. The Normans had attacked the Saxon encampment with the utmost impetuosity in front and in flank. The Saxons maintained their ground well, but some, through fear or misadventure, were constrained to flee. The victorious Normans, strongly armed and well mounted, pursued the flying footmen. In doing so, they left not only their own army, but that of Harold in the rear. Soon a swampy valley was to be encountered. The retreating English, climbing the opposite hill, paused, at once to take breath and to examine their position. Finding the Normans struggling with the difficulties of the morass, and conscious of the advantage which their elevated position gave them, they wheeled about, and became the attacking party. Their efforts were crowned with success; the invaders were thrown into a state of confusion nearly inextricable. But it is necessary now to refer to our authorities. The account given in the *Roman de Rou* of this important part of the events of that eventful day is the following : " In the plain was a fosse, which the Normans now had behind them, *having passed it in the fight without regarding it.* But the English charged, and drove the Normans before them, till they made them fall back upon this fosse, overthrowing into it horses and men. Many were to be seen falling therein, rolling one over the other, with their faces to the earth, and unable to rise. Many of the English also, whom the Normans drew down along with them, died there. At no time during the day's battle did so many Normans die as perished in that fosse. So said they who saw the dead." The account given in the *Chronicle of Battle Abbey* is similar. " There lay between the hostile armies a certain dreadful precipice......It was of considerable extent, and being overgrown with bushes or brambles, was not very easily seen, and great numbers of men, principally Normans in pursuit of the English, were suffocated in it. For, ignorant of the danger, as they were running in a disorderly manner, they fell into the chasm, and were fearfully

T

dashed to pieces and slain. And this pit, from this deplorable accident, is still called *Malfosse*." With these statements that of William of Malmesbury agrees—"By frequently making a stand, they slaughtered their pursuers in heaps; for, getting possession of an eminence, they drove down the Normans, when roused with indignation and anxiously striving to gain the higher ground, into the valley beneath, when, easily hurling their javelins and rolling down stones on them as they stood below, they destroyed them to a man." With these descriptions the delineation of the Tapestry agrees in a remarkable manner. The only point which remains for us is to identify the scene of this skirmish with some locality in the vicinity of Battle. This Mr. Lower enables us to do. "There is no place near Battle which can, with a due regard to the proprieties of language, be called a 'dreadful precipice' *(miserabile præcipitium vaste patens)*, though, by comparing Malmesbury with the Monk of Battle, I think I have succeeded in identifying the locality of this 'bad ditch.'[a] From all the probabilities of the case, it would seem that the flight and pursuit must have lain in a north-westerly direction, through that part of the district known as Mountjoy. Assuming this, the eminence alluded to must have been the ridge rising from Mount Street to Caldbeck Hill, and the *Malfosse* some part of the stream which, flowing at its feet, runs in the direction of Watlington, and becomes a tributary of the Rother. This rivulet occasionally overflows its banks, and the primitive

[a] On accompanying Mr. Lower to the spot, in January, 1853, I was satisfied of the correctness of his views.

condition of the adjacent levels was doubtless that of a morass, overgrown with flags, reeds, and similar bog vegetables. Thanks, however, to good drainage, this ' bad ditch' no longer remains. The name was corrupted, previously to 1279, to Manfosse, and a piece of land called Wincestrecroft, in Manfosse, was ceded to the Abbey of Battle in that year. Now Wincestrecroft is still well known, and lies in the direction specified, west by north of the present town of Battle.''[a]

The English, after having exterminated their pursuers, regained the eminence on which the main body was encamped.

This was the most critical period of the day's fight. The varlets who had been set to guard the harness of the Normans, began to abandon it. The priests who had confessed and blessed the army in the morning, and had meanwhile retired to a neighbouring height, began to take themselves off. In this extremity Odo interfered, and turned the fate of the battle. The description in the *Roman de Rou* precisely corresponds with the drawing in the Tapestry. Wace says, " Then Odo, the good priest, the Bishop of Bayeux, galloped up, and said to them ' Stand fast, stand fast ! be quiet and move not ! fear nothing, for if it please God, we shall conquer yet.' So they took courage, and rested where they were ; and Odo returned galloping back to where the battle was most fierce, and was of great service on that day. He had put a hauberk on, over a white aube, wide in the body, with the sleeves tight ; and sat on a white horse, so that all might recognize him.

[a] Sussex Archæological Collections, vol. vi., p. 27.

In his hand he held a mace, and wherever he saw most need, he led up and stationed the knights, and often urged them on to assault and strike the enemy." With this description the Tapestry exactly accords, except in the colour of the horse; it however represents it as being sufficiently conspicuous.

The inscription is HIC ODO EPISCOPUS TENENS BACULUM CONFORTAT PUEROS—Here Odo holding a staff exhorts the soldiers.[a] The staff which Odo wields is, I suspect, the badge of command—the marshal's baton as it were—and not a weapon, as some writers suppose. William himself, in the next group, is represented with a similar implement. During the middle ages the priests of the sanctuary were not unfrequently to be found in the battle-field. Some of them were much more at home in the midst of the *melée* than in guiding sin-stricken souls to a Saviour. The bold Bishop of Durham, Anthony Beck, never left the precincts of his castle but in magnificent military array. He fought personally at the battle of Falkirk, and drew from a soldier, who felt perhaps a superstitious dread at aiming a deadly blow at one invested with the sacred office, the merited rebuke, " To your mass, O priest." Richard I., when at war with Philip of France, took a

---

[a] There has been a discussion respecting the word *pueros,* some supposing that the parties thus addressed were young soldiers, inexperienced recruits. It is probable, however, that the word is equivalent to the phrase, " lads" among us, or the word " *boys*" in the lines which carried so much terror to the heart of James the Second, after he had seen a specimen of the stalwart youth which Cornwall produces—

" And must Trelawney die, and must Trelawney die ?
Then twenty thousand Cornish *boys* will ask the reason why."

French Bishop prisoner. The Pope sent to demand his liberation, claiming him as a son of the church. Richard upon this sent the Bishop's coat of mail to the Pope, just as it was, besmeared with the blood of the slain, employing the words of Jacob's sons, "This have we found; know now whether it be thy son's coat or no." The canon laws indeed forbade a priest to shed blood; but this was evaded, it is said, by the use of a mace instead of a sword. The warrior-priest did not stab a man; he only brained him. It is on this ground that the baton held by Odo has been considered by some writers to be a weapon.

In consequence of the confusion and panic which attended the disasters in the Malfosse, a report was spread among the Normans that William was dead. At the same time, too, according to one writer,[a] Eustace Count of Boulogne strongly urged the Duke to withdraw his forces from the field, considering the battle to be lost beyond recovery. A Saxon shaft at that moment laid Eustace low, and delivered William from his importunity. The Duke, nothing daunted by this disaster, rushed among his troops, encouraged his men to maintain the combat, and to assure them of the falsehood of the report of his death, raised his helmet and exhibited himself to his people. This act is exhibited in the Tapestry *(Plate XXX)*; at the same time, his standard-bearer, who never left him throughout the day, draws attention to the circumstance. The group is labelled, HIC EST DVX WILEL :—Here is Duke William. By these energetic means the Normans returned to the onset.

[a] Benoit de Saint-More. Taylor's Wace, 193.

The Tapestry shows us the fearful slaughter which took place on that hard-fought field. The border is filled with dead men and horses lying in every conceivable position; a head is not unfrequently deposited at some distance from the body to which it once belonged. We can scarcely look upon the drawing without being impressed with the idea that the designer of the Tapestry had been the witness of some fight. It is said that when a man receives a mortal wound, his body is thrown for the moment into violent spasmodic action. So much is this the case, that you may tell the effect of a death-bringing volley by noticing how many unhappy wretches make a sudden leap. In the Tapestry something of this spasmodic action is manifested, and some of the men are coming to the ground in such a posture as they could only do after having sprung up from it.[a]

The battle had now lasted the greater part of the day. " From nine o'clock in the morning till three in the afternoon the battle was up and down, this way and that, and no one knew who would conquer and win the land. Both sides stood so firm and fought so

[a] The special correspondent of *The Times*, writing from the Heights of Alma, Sep. 21st, 1854, says, " The attitudes of some of the dead were awful. One man might be seen resting on one knee, with the arms extended in the form of taking aim, the brow compressed, the lips clinched—the very expression of firing at an enemy stamped on the face and fixed there by death; a ball had struck this man in the neck. Physiologists or anatomists must settle the rest. Another was lying on his back with the same expression, and his arms raised in a similar attitude, the Minié musket still grasped in his hands undischarged. *Another lay in a perfect arch, his head resting on one part of the ground and his feet on the other, but his back raised high above it.—The Times*, Oct. 11th, 1854. *See* also Sir Charles Bell's *Anatomy of Expression*, 3rd edition, p. 160.

well that no one could guess which would prevail. The Norman archers with their bows shot thickly upon the English; but they covered themselves with their shields, so that the arrows could not reach their bodies......Then the Normans determined to shoot their arrows upwards into the air, so that they might fall on their enemies' heads and strike their faces. The archers adopted this scheme, and shot up into the air towards the English; and the arrows in falling struck their heads and faces, and put out the eyes of many, and all feared to open their eyes or leave their faces unguarded." "The arrows now flew thicker than rain before the wind. Then it was that an arrow that had been thus shot upwards struck Harold above his right eye and put it out. In his agony he drew the arrow *(Plate XXXI.)* and threw it away, breaking it with his hands; and the pain to his head was so great that he leaned upon his shield." Still the English did not yield, and Harold, though grievously hurt, maintained his ground.

At length the device was adopted which put victory into the hands of the Normans. Harold, knowing William's skill in strategy, exhorted his troops at the beginning of the fight to keep their ground, and not suffer themselves to be drawn into a pursuit. Had his troops been well-trained men, to whom obedience is a second nature, that battle had probably not been lost. Many of them however had been brought from the fields, and were unable to resist the prospect of inflicting deserved vengeance upon their adversaries. Harold's troops were the more likely to fall into the snare laid for them, in consequence of the success which attended, in an earlier part of the day, the attack upon the pursuing Normans in the Malfosse.

William's army fled by little and little, the English following them. " As the one fell back, the other pressed after ; and when the Frenchmen retreated, the English thought and cried out that the men of France fled and would never return. ' Cowards,' said they, ' you came hither in an evil hour, wanting our lands, and seeking to seize our property, fools that you were to come ! Normandy is too far off, and you will not easily reach it....your sons and daughters are lost to you !' The Normans bore these taunts very quietly, as indeed they easily might, for they did not know what the English said."

At length the time arrived for the assailants to come to a stand. The English had broken rank ; the valley, too, had been crossed, and the Normans were now standing above the Saxons on the flank of the hill on the top of which they had formed in the morning.

At the word of command, DEX AIE, the Normans halted, and turned their faces towards the enemey. Now commenced the fiercest part of that bloody day's encounter. Neither party was wanting in courage. All the chroniclers do justice to the contending forces. " One hits, another misses ; one flies, another pursues ; one is aiming a stroke, while another discharges his blow. Norman strives with Englishman again, and aims his blows afresh. One flies, another pursues swiftly ; the combatants are many, the plain wide, the battle and the *melée* fierce. On every hand they fight hard, the blows are heavy, and the struggle becomes fierce."

As neither the horrors nor the gallantry exhibited on a battle-field can be comprehended by a general description, it may be well here to introduce an account of one or two of the individual encounters occurring at this period, with which Wace supplies us.

" The Normans were playing their part well, when an English knight came rushing up, having in his company a hundred men furnished with various arms. He wielded a northern hatchet, with the blade a full foot long; and was well armed after his manner, being tall, bold, and of noble carriage. In the front of the battle, where the Normans thronged most, he came bounding on swifter than a stag, many Normans falling before him and his company. He rushed straight upon a Norman, who was armed, and riding on a war-horse, and tried with a hatchet of steel to cleave his helmet; but the blow miscarried, and the sharp blade glanced down before the saddle-bow, driving through the horse's neck down to the ground, so that both horse and master fell together to the earth. I know not whether the Englishman struck another blow; but the Normans who saw the stroke were astonished, and about to abandon the assault, when Roger de Montgomery came galloping up, with his lance set, and heeding not the long-handled axe which the Englishman wielded aloft, struck him down, and left him stretched upon the ground. Then Roger cried out ' Frenchmen, strike; the day is ours !' And again a fierce *melée* was to be seen, with many a blow of lance and sword; the English still defending themselves, killing the horses, and cleaving the shields."

" There was a French soldier of noble mien, who sat his horse

U

gallantly.   He spied two Englishmen who were also carrying themselves boldly.   They were both of them men of great worth, and had become companions in arms and fought together, the one protecting the other.   They bore two long and broad bills, and did great mischief to the Normans, killing both horses and men.   The French soldier looked at them and their bills, and was sore alarmed; for he was afraid of losing his good horse, the best that he had, and would willingly have turned to some other quarter, if it would not have looked like cowardice.   Fearing the two bills, he raised his shield by the ' enarmes,' and struck one of the Englishmen with his lance on the breast, so that the iron passed out at the back."   At the moment that he fell, the lance broke, and the Frenchman seized the mace that hung at his right side, and struck the other Englishman a blow that completely fractured his scull."

The slaughter at this period of the day must have been fearful. The chronicler of Battle Abbey says, " Amid these miseries there was exhibited a fearful spectacle : the fields were covered with dead bodies, and on every hand nothing was to be seen but the red hue of blood.   The dales around sent forth a gory stream, which increased at a distance to the size of a river !   How great think you must have been the slaughter of the conquered, when the conquerors' is reported, upon the lowest computation, to have exceeded ten thousand ?   Oh how vast a flood of human gore was poured out in that place where these unfortunates fell and were slain !   What a dashing to pieces of arms, what a clashing of strokes ; what shrieks of dying men ; what grief ; what sighs were heard ! How many groans ; how many bitter notes of direst calamity then sounded forth, who can rightly calculate ! What a wretched exhibition of human misery was there to call forth astonishment ! In the very contemplation of it our heart fails us."[a]

Notwithstanding the horrors of the scene, and the hopelessness of their efforts, the courage of the Saxons failed not ; sometimes fleeing, and sometimes making a stand, they slaughtered their pursuers in heaps.

The place where this havoc took place is probably the southern front of the eminence on which Battle Abbey was afterwards placed. The whole site of the contest has sometimes been denominated " Sanguelac," or the " Lake of Blood," but this designation properly belongs to that part in which the street of the modern town of Battle called " the Lake" is situated. Until a very recent period this place was supposed still occasionally to reek with human gore. " Thereabout," says Drayton, " is a place which after rain always looks red, which some have attributed to a very bloody sweat of the earth, as crying to heaven for revenge for so great a slaughter."

> " .... Asten once distained with native English blood;
> Whose soil, when wet with any little rain,
> Doth blush, as put in mind of those there sadly slain."

The truth is " the redness of the water here, and at many other places in the neighbourhood, is caused by the oxydation of the iron which abounds in the soil of the Weald of Sussex."[b]

[a] M. A. Lower's Battle Abbey Chronicle, p. 7.   [b] Ibid.

To return to the battle, "Loud was now the clamour, and great the slaughter; many a soul then quitted the body which it inhabited. The living marched over the heaps of dead, and each side was weary of striking. He charged on who could, and he who could no longer strike still pushed forward. The strong struggled with the strong; some failed, others triumphed; the cowards fell back, the brave pressed on; and sad was his fate who fell in the midst, for he had little chance of rising again; and many in truth fell who never rose at all, being crushed under the throng. And now the Normans pressed on so far that at last they reached the English standard." The Tapestry represents the eager advance of a body of horsemen. The compartment is inscribed, HIC FRANCI PUGNANT ET CECIDERUNT QUI ERANT CUM HAROLDO—Here the French are fighting, and have slain the men who were with Harold. "There Harold had remained, defending himself to the utmost; but he was sorely wounded in the eye by the arrow, and suffered grievous pain by the blow. An armed man came in the throng of the battle, and struck him on the *ventaille* of his helmet and beat him to the ground; and as he sought to recover himself, a knight beat him down again, striking him on the thick of his thigh, down to the bone." This is shown in the Tapestry *(Plate XXXII)* Harold first of all appears standing by his standard, contending with a horseman who is making a rush at him; then he is shown pulling the arrow out of his eye; and lastly he is seen, falling—

"With his back to the field, and his feet to the foe,"

—his battle axe has dropped from his nerveless grasp, and a Norman, stooping from his horse, inflicts a wound upon his thigh. The group is superscribed, HIC HAROLD REX INTERFECTUS EST— Here Harold the King is slain.[a]

" The English were in great trouble at having lost their King, and at the Duke's having conquered and beat down the standard; but they still fought on, and defended themselves long, and in fact till the day drew to a close. Then it clearly appeared to all that the standard was lost, and the news had spread throughout the army that Harold for certain was dead; and all saw now that there was no longer any hope, so they left the field and those fled who could." Ingulph tells us that all the nobles that were in Harold's army were slain;[b] we are hence led to infer that it was the untrained peasantry only who betook themselves to flight. The Tapestry is in consistency with this. The last compartment represents a group of men unprotected by body armour, and supplied only with a mace or club, retreating before a party of fully equipped horsemen. The inscription is, ET FUGA VERTERUNT ANGLI —And the English betake themselves to flight.

Happily the exact spot on which the final struggle of the day took place is clearly ascertained. The writer of the *Battle Abbey*

[a] The Tapestry represents the death of Harold as rapidly succeeding the infliction of the wound in his eye. The impression left by a perusal of Wace is, that at least an hour or two elapsed between the one event and the other. The diversity of statement between these authorities is probably more apparent than real. After Harold was wounded in so important an organ as the eye, it was impossible that he could long withstand the onset of William's troops; his defeat, or, in other words, his death, was certain. However manfully Harold may have borne up under the inconvenience and pain of his wound, the artist of the Tapestry is logically correct in at once bringing us to the conclusion of the scene.

[b] Ingulph's Chronicle, p. 139.

Chronicle tells us, that the King having resolved to commemorate his victory by the erection of a Christian temple, the high altar was placed upon the precise spot where the standard was observed to fall.[a] Long after all traces of the Abbey Church had been obliterated, the finger of tradition faithfully pointed to the spot so interesting to all Englishmen. In the year 1817, the proprietor of the soil, anxious to test the truth of the popular belief, made the necessary excavations, and in the very place indicated, at the depth of several feet below the surface, found the remains of an altar in the easternmost recess of the crypt of the church.[b]

William on that day fought well—as well he might, for he had engaged in a desperate venture—" many a blow did he give, and many receive, and many fell dead under his hand." Two horses were killed under him. After the English had been exterminated, or had forsaken the field, the Duke returned thanks to God, and ordered his gonfanon to be erected where Harold's standard had stood. Here, too, he raised his tent. Amidst the dying and the dead he partook of his evening meal and passed the night.

The next morning which dawned upon that sad battle field was the Sabbath. On that first day of the week no heavenly choir sang of peace on earth and good will toward men. The human family

[a] Lower's Chronicle of Battle Abbey; p. 11.

[b] Sussex Archæological Collections, vol. 1., page 33.—For some years the public have been admitted to the Abbey grounds only on one day of the week, and that the day (Monday) most inconvenient to those who reside at a distance from Battle. Let us hope that henceforth no one respectfully requesting permission to muse upon the spot where the deed was done on which the modern history of the world has turned, will meet with a denial.

was exhibited in its most painful aspect, "hateful and hating one another"—that field but recently covered over with the golden sheaves of harvest, now bore upon its surface the gory fruits of man's ambition.

"When William called over the muster-roll, which he had prepared before he left the opposite coast, many a knight, who on the day when he sailed, had proudly answered to his name, was then numbered with the dead. The land which he had done homage for was useless to him now."[a] He had come to win large domains and baronial honours—six feet of common earth was all he got. "The Conqueror had lost more than one-fourth of his army."[b] Both parties spent the day in burying the dead. "The noble ladies of the land also came, some to seek their husbands, and others their fathers, sons, or brothers."

The account given by Ordericus of the disposal of Harold's body is the following: "Harold could not be discovered by his features, but was recognized by other tokens, and his corpse being borne to the Duke's camp, was, by order of the Conqueror, delivered to William Mallet for interment near the sea-shore, which had long been guarded by his arms."[c] William of Poictiers gives a similar statement. Later writers say that his body was interred with regal honours in Waltham Abbey. This tradition, which probably had its origin in the wish of the monks to attract visitors to the shrine at Waltham, cannot be entertained, in opposition to the express

[a] History of the Anglo-Saxons (European Library,)p. 337.
[b] Lingard's Hist. Eng., vol. i., p. 313.
[c] Vol. i., p. 487.

statements of contemporaries. Some venture, too, to assert that, though sorely wounded at Hastings, he was not killed, and that, on escaping from the field, he first fled to the continent, and afterwards led the life of a recluse at Chester. This is a statement which may at once be rejected.

The difficulty in discovering the body to which Ordericus refers was, it is generally believed, overcome by Edith, surnamed, from her beauty, the Fair. The keen eye of affection discerned his mangled form amidst heaps of dead, which appeared to common observers an undistinguishable mass. What will not woman's love accomplish!

Many writers have done great dishonour to this lady by stating that she was the mistress of Harold. Sir Henry Ellis, in his *Introduction to Domesday Book*, has proved that she was his Queen; "Aldith, Algiva or Eddeva, being names which are all synonymous." Unhappy Elfgyva, how different her feelings now from what they were when the clerk announced to her, in his own familiar way, the rescue of Harold from the capture of Guy!

IX. THE SEQUEL.

"From seeming evil still educing good."
Thomson.

THE Saxons lost the battle of Hastings. Here, however, they left no blot on their name. The old historian Daniel justly, as well as forcibly, remarks, "Thus was tried, by the great assize of God's judgment in battle, the right of power between the English and Norman nations; a battle the most memorable of all others; and, however miserably lost, yet most nobly fought on the part of England." The death of Harold, and the absence of any other competitor, opened the way for William to the throne. Presenting himself to the nobles of the land, assembled in London, he was in due form elected to the vacant throne, and was crowned by Aldred Archbishop of York, on Mid-winter's day. William never claimed the English crown by right of conquest. His quarrel was with Harold, not with the English people, and he denounced him as interfering with his just claims. The *Saxon Chronicle* expressly asserts that "Before the Archbishop would set the crown upon his head, he required of him a pledge upon Christ's book, and also swore him, that he would govern this nation as well as any king before him had at the best done, if they would be faithful to him." He never claimed to be the Conqueror of England in the ordinary

W

sense of the word. In his first charter to Westminster Abbey, he founds his right to the crown upon the grant of his relative Edward the Confessor. The *Domesday Book* was not compiled until near the close of William's reign (about the year 1086), yet in it he is not spoken of as a conqueror. "Throughout the *Survey*," says Sir Henry Ellis, "Harold is constantly spoken of as the usurper of the realm: 'quando regnum *invasit.*' Once only is it said 'quando *regnabat.*' Of William it is as constantly said, 'postquam *venit* in Angliam,' after he came to England. Once only does the expression occur, 'W. rex *conquisivit* Angliam,' when he conquered or acquired England."[a] But whatever were William's rights and original intentions, it was impossible that he could long reign over England as a constitutional monarch. It was not likely that the great chiefs who survived the battle of Hastings would long submit to the rule of a stranger—hosts of foreigners would necessarily be introduced into the court, and this, as in the reign of the Confessor, would be a continual source of heartburning and jealousy —and, above all, the followers of the King were to be rewarded, and this could only be done by depriving the Saxon noblemen of their patrimonies. When William won the battle of Hastings, he bid farewell to peace for ever. His subsequent history was a continued series of entanglements and broils. One chieftain after another, one district and then another, became restless under his rule ; each

---

[a] General Introduction to Domesday, vol. i. p. 311. In all probability William obtained the title of Conqueror from the Latin word *conquiro*, which in its legal acceptation signified to acquire. It is still used in this sense by the Scottish lawyers.

he crushed in succession. At length he became in the strict sense of the word the Conqueror. He ruled by the sword alone. His own Norman barons, and even his brother Odo, felt the weight of his iron hand; but it fell with peculiar force upon his native-born subjects. The writer in the *Saxon Chronicle*, speaking from his own knowledge, says of William, " He was a very wise and a great man, and more honoured and more powerful than any of his predecessors. He was mild to those good men who loved God, but severe beyond measure towards those who withstood his will.......He was a very stern and wrathful man, so that none durst do anything against his will, and he kept in prison those earls who acted against his pleasure.......Truly there was much trouble in these times, and very great distress; he caused castles to be built, and oppressed the poor.......He made large forests for the deer, and enacted laws therewith, so that whoever killed a hart or a hind should be blinded. He loved the tall stags as if he had been their father. The rich complained and the poor murmured, but he was so sturdy that he recked nought of them; they must will all that the king willed, if they would live; or would keep their lands; or would hold their possessions; or would be maintained in their rights. Alas! that any man should so exalt himself, and carry himself in his pride over all!"[a] Ingulph speaks of the entire subjugation of the English people, and of their systematic exclusion from offices of honour. " Many of the chief men of the land, for some time, offered resistance to William, the new

[a] Saxon Chronicle, Bohn's edition, p. 462.

king, but, being afterwards crushed by his might and overcome, they at last submitted to the sway of the Normans. ...... So inveterately did the Normans at this period detest the English, that, whatever the amount of their merits might be, they were excluded from all dignities; and foreigners who were far less fitted, be they of any other nation whatever under heaven, would have been gladly chosen instead of them."[a] Henry of Huntingdon uses language which the English of the present day, accustomed as they are to rear their heads proudly among the nations, can hardly understand. "In the twenty-first year of the reign of King William, when the Normans had accomplished the righteous will of God on the English Nation, and there was now no prince of the ancient regal race living in England, and all the English were brought to a reluctant submission, so that *it was a disgrace even to be called an Englishman*, the instrument of Providence in fulfilling its designs was removed from the world."[b] "Many of the people," as Holinshed tells us, "utterly refusing such an intolerable yoke of thraldom as was daily laid upon them, chose rather to leave all, both goods and lands, and after the manner of outlaws, got them to the woods with their wives, children, and servants, meaning from henceforth to live upon the spoils of the country adjoining, and to take whatsoever came next to hand."

Notwithstanding the heavy pressure of these evils good ensued. The political tempest resulted in the increased purity, health, and peace, of the national atmosphere.

[a] Ingulph's Chronicle, p. 140.   [b] Henry of Huntingdon, vol. i. p. 216.

William established a strong government. Had Harold been unopposed from without, he would have had rivals from within the nation. The opposition of his own brother Tostig was but a prelude of what the general result of his reign would have been. Ambitious men, such as Edwin and Morcar, the Earls of Mercia and Northumbria, would on the least provocation have espoused the cause of Edgar Atheling, and by rendering the land a scene of internal discord, have made it an easy prey to new bands of adventurers from Denmark, Norway, Flanders. and France. William, by the vigour, and even harshness of his rule, quelled internal dissension, and bid defiance to foreign rivalry.

The Norman invasion hastened and perfected the establishment of the feudal system in England. This system had one great defect, which renders it unfit for the present condition of England— it altogether overlooked the claims of the lower classes, who always form the great bulk of the population ; still, it produced most beneficial results in the eleventh and twelfth centuries. It brought all the great barons of the empire into subjection to the sovereign, and by defining the corresponding duties of the mesne lords and inferior tenants, knit the whole kingdom into one. By this unity the realm was prepared to put down intestine broils, and to resist foreign aggression. A way too was prepared for the elevation of the lower classes. The system had but to be extended in order to define the duties, and to confer corresponding privileges, upon every member of the community.

Learning and civilization were greatly advanced by the Norman Conquest. Italy at this time was the focus of the knowledge and refinement of the world. The light kindled by the genius of Attica, and nurtured by the philosophy and poetry of the Augustan era, still irradiated the seven-hilled city. Britain, severed from the main-land by a stormy channel, had less intercourse with Rome than the nations of the continent. Though William of Malmesbury may have somewhat overdrawn the statement, still there is much truth in the picture which he gives of the social condition of the Saxons at the time of the Conquest. " In process of time the desire after literature and religion had decayed, for several years before the arrival of the Normans. The clergy, contented with a very slight degree of learning, could scarcely stammer out the words of the sacraments; and a person who understood grammar was an object of wonder and astonishment. The nobility were given up to luxury and wantonness. The commonalty, left unprotected, became a prey to the most powerful, who amassed fortunes, by either seizing on their property, or by selling their persons into foreign countries; although it be an innate quality of this people to be more inclined to revelling, than to the accumulation of wealth. Drinking was a universal practice, in which they passed entire nights as well as days. They consumed their whole substance in mean and despicable houses; unlike Normans and French, who, in noble and splendid mansions, lived with frugality."[a] There cannot be a doubt that by the introduction of the refinements of life the condition of the people was improved,

[a] William of Malmesbury, p. 279.

and that a check was given to the grosser sensualities of our nature. Certain it is that learning received a powerful stimulus by the conquest. At the period of the Norman invasion, a great intellectual movement had commenced in the schools on the continent. Normandy had beyond most other parts profited by it. William brought with him to England some of the most distinguished ornaments of the schools of his native duchy; the consequence of this was that England henceforward took a higher walk in literature than she had ever done before.[a]

Another important advantage resulting from the Conquest was the emancipation of the lower classes. At the period of the invasion the great bulk of the population were in a servile condition. One class of the people, the churls, were attached to the land, and were transferred with it from one master to another without the power of choosing their employer, or taking any steps to improve their condition—another large class, the thews, were the absolute property of their owners. The attempts which Alfred and some of the clergy made to remedy this gigantic evil were attended with but partial success. The Conquest gave it its death blow. The convulsions which ensued afforded great numbers the wished-for opportunity of escaping from thraldom. Many of the landowners, seeing the shipwreck of their fortunes inevitable, made a virtue of necessity, and manumitted their serfs. One of William's regulations had a tendency quietly to complete what was thus auspiciously begun. He passed a law declaring that every slave who

[a] *See* Wright's Biographia Britannica, vol. ii., p. 10.

had resided unchallenged a year and a day in any city or walled town in the kingdom, should be free for ever.[a] This law became a door of hope to many, and in due time not one slave was left in England. It had another very beneficial effect. Men were led to congregate in towns; knowledge was promoted; a stimulus was given to the cultivation of the refinements of social life; and the commoners, strong in their numbers, were induced to assert and maintain their common rights.

Even the despotic measures of the king had a beneficial influence upon the lower grades of society. The thanes and aldermen of the Confessor's days being deprived of their lands, were glad to hold a small portion of them as the inferior tenants of the great Norman barons. Hence sprung the yeomanry of England, who, in days of difficulty and danger, have often proved themselves the mainstay of the country. The Saxon noblemen, in descending from their high estate, brought with them their independence of feeling and high spirit. They were chastened but not crushed. They not only maintained their own freedom of thought, but infused a portion of their energy into the newly emancipated class below them. Formerly the difference in social position between the landed proprietor and the tiller of the soil was so great, that there could be little friendly intercourse between them, and no unity of interest; but now, by the formation of a middle class, the two extremes of society were linked together, and all classes placed in a position to benefit the rest, as well as to be benefited by them.

[a] Would not the United States of America do well to notice this?

The hope of rising in the social scale now dawned upon the lower orders.

Another signal benefit resulted from the Conquest. It brought to our English soil a host of men renowned in their own persons and those of their descendants for all that is great in art and arms, for all that is noble in knightly enterprise and chivalric feeling. Strike out from the page of history the deeds of the Montfords, the Marmions, the Warrens, the Nevilles, the Percys, the Beauchamps, the Bruces, the Balliols, the Talbots, the Cliffords, and a host of others who fought with William at Hastings, or followed in his wake, what a blank would be left. True, they were not always found contending on the side of liberty and truth; but, on the whole, they contributed to the developement of England's liberties and enlightenment and power, and left an example of indomitable energy and manly bearing which mankind to the latest ages will do well to copy.

One other view of the subject we must take. England required chastisement, but shall the oppressor on that account go free? The chroniclers most favourable to William do not conceal the harshness and covetousness which disfigured the latter part of his reign. They tell us, too, of the evils which afflicted his age, and pursued him beyond the tomb. His eldest son rose in rebellion against him. Many of his own nobles joined the undutiful youth; even his beloved wife Matilda favoured him. In the New Forest, which he had wrongfully appropriated to his own pleasures, his son Richard was slain, during his lifetime. His son William,

x

who succeeded him, came to a violent end in the same place. A grandson also is said to have perished in it. Whilst ravaging Mantes, in revenge for an idle jest, he met with his own death stroke. No sooner had he ceased to breathe than his lifeless body was forsaken by his family and domestics. When all that remained of the once potent William was about to be committed to the tomb, the man from whom he had wrested the site forbade his burial; some of the bystanders 'of their charity' satisfied the claim, and the Conqueror was laid in an eleemosynary grave. At a subsequent period that grave was violated, and his bones dispersed.

His followers, bent upon enriching themselves at the expense of justice, did not escape. Many of them rose in rebellion, and were crushed. Others suffered in the troubles which ensued upon his death. In the struggle between Stephen and Matilda, dreadful was the havoc committed upon the followers of William and their children. During the Wars of the Roses, nearly all the great families founded at the Conquest suffered calamities differing little in kind or degree from those which the victors of Hastings inflicted upon the old nobility of the land. History gives emphasis to the divine injunction, " Fret not thyself because of evil doers, neither be thou envious against the workers of iniquity: for they shall soon be cut down like the grass, and wither as the green herb."

APPENDIX.

NOTE A.—*Page 4.*

The authority for the odd story of the Duke of Normandy's courtship is the following passage in the *Chronicle of Tours,* quoted in the *Encyclopædia Metropolitana,* Vol. xi., p. 527, *n.*

"Tunc Guillelmus, Dux Normanniæ, Mathildam, filiam Balduini Comitis Flandriæ duxit in uxorem in hunc modum. Cum ipsa a Patre suo de sponso recipiendo sæpius rogaretur, eique Guillelmus Normannicus a Patre, qui eum longo tempore nutrierat, præ aliis laudaretur, respondit, nunquam Nothum recipere se maritum. Quo audito, Guillelmus Dux clam apud Brugis, ubi puella morabatur, cum paucis accelerat, eamque, regredientem ab Ecclesiâ pugnis, calcibus, atque calcaribus verberet atque castigat, sicque ascenso equo in patriam remeat. Quo facto, puella dolens ad lectum decubat; ad quam Pater veniens illam de sponso recipiendo interrogat et requirit; quæ respondens dixit se nunquam habere maritum nisi Guillelmum Ducem Normanniæ; quod et factum est."

NOTE B.—*Page 5.*

As the following letter of M. Thierry's is less accessible to the English reader than most of the documents connected with the Bayeux Tapestry it is here given in full. It is addressed to M. de la Fontenelle de Vaudoré :—

"Monsieur,—Pardonnez-moi de répondre bien tard à une demande qui, venant de vous, m'honore infiniment. Vous désirez savoir ce que je pense des *Recherches et conjectures* de M. Bolton Corney *sur la tapisserie de Bayeux ;* je vais vous le dire, en aussi peu de mots et aussi nettement que je le pourrai. L'opinion soutenue par M. Bolton Corney comprend deux thèses principales : 1° que la tapisserie de Bayeux n'est pas un don de la reine Mathilde, ni même un don fait au chapitre de cette ville par un autre personne; qu'elle a été fabriqué pour l'église cathédrale de Bayeux, sur l'ordre et aux frais du chapitre; 2° que ce vénérable monument n'est pas contemporain de la conquête de l'Angleterre par les Normands, mais qu'il date du temps où la Normandie se trouvait réunie à la France. De ces deux thèses, la première me semble vraie de toute évidence, la seconde est inadmissible.

" La tradition qui attribuait à la reine Mathilde la pièce de tapisserie conservée à Bayeux, tradition, du reste, assez récente, et que l'abbé de La Rue a réfutée, n'est plus soutenue par personne. Quant à la seconde question, celle de savoir si cette tapisserie fut ou non un présent fait à l'église de Bayeux, M. Bolton Corney la résout négativement, et d'une façon qui me semble péremptoire. Au silence des anciens inventaires de l'église il joint des preuves tirées du monument lui-même, et démontre avec évidence que ses détails portent une empreinte très-marquée de localité, que la conquête de l'Angleterre par les Normands y a été considérée en quelque sorte au point de vue de la ville et de l'église de Bayeux. Un seul évêque y figure, et c'est celui de Bayeux, très-souvent en scène et quelquefois désigné par son seul titre : *episcopus*. De plus, parmi les personnages laïques qui figurent à côté du duc Guillaume, pas un ne porte un nom historique. Les noms qui reviennent sans cesse sont ceux de Turold, Wadard et Vital, probablement connus et chéris à Bayeux, car les deux derniers, Wadard et Vital, sont inscrits sur le Domesday-Book, au nombre des feudataires de l'église de Bayeux, dans les comtés de Kent, d'Oxford, et de Lincoln. Si l'on joint à ces raisons celles que M. Bolton Corney déduit de la forme et de l'usage particuliers du monument, il est impossible de ne pas croire avec lui que là tapisserie fut commandée par le chapitre de Bayeux et exécutée pour lui.

" Je passe à la seconde proposition, savoir que la tapisserie de Bayeux fut exécutée après la réunion de la Normandie à la France. Cette hypothèse n'exige pas une longue réfutation, car l'auteur du mémoire la fonde sur une seule preuve, l'emploi du mot *Franci* pour désigner l'armée normande. 'Guillaume de Poitiers, dit-il, appelle ceux qui faisaient partie de l'armée *Normanni*, des Normands ; la tapisserie les nomme toujours *Franci*, des Français. Je considère cela comme une bévue indicative du temps où le monument a été exécute.' Il n'y a là aucune bévue, ni rien qui puisse faire présumer que la tapisserie de Bayeux n'est pas contemporaine de la conquête de l'Angleterre par les Normands. En effet, les Anglo-Saxons avaient coutume de désigner par le nom de Français *(Frencan, Frencisce men)* tous les habitants de la Gaule, sans distinction de province ou d'origine. La Chronique saxonne, dans les mille endroits où elle parle des chefs et des soldats de l'armée normande, les appelle Français. Ce nom servait en Angleterre à distinguer les conquérants de la population indigène, non-seulement dans le langage usuel, mais encore dans celui des acts légaux. On lit dans les lois de Guillaume-le-Conquérant, à l'article du meurtre, ces mots : *Ki Franceis occist*, et, dans la version latine de ces lois :

Si Francigena interfectus fuerit. L'emploi du mot *Franci* au lieu de *Normanni*, ne prouve donc point que la tapisserie de Bayeux date d'un temps posterieur à la conquête. S'il prouve quelque chose, c'est que la tapisserie a été exécutée non en Normandie, mais en Angleterre, et que c'est à des ouvriers ou ouvrières de ce dernier pays que le chapitre de Bayeux a fait sa commande.

"Cette opinion, que je soumets au jugement des archéologues, est confirmée d'ailleurs par l'orthographe de certains mots et par l'emploi de certaines lettres dans les légendes du monument. On y trouve, jusque dans le nom du duc Guilluame et dans celui de la ville de Bayeux, des traces de prononciation anglo-saxonne : *Hic Wido adduxit Haroldum ad Wilgelmum normannorum ducem ; Willém venit Bagias ;* c'est le *g* saxon qui figure ici avec sa consonance *hié*. *Wilgelm* pour *Wilielm, Bagias* pour *Bayeux*. La dipthongue *ea*, l'une des particularités de l'orthographe anglo-saxon, se rencontre dans les légendes qui offrent le nom du roi Edward : *Hic portatur corpus* EADWARDI. Une autre légende présente cette indication de lieu, correctement saxonne : *Ut foderetur castellum at* HESTENCA CASTRA. Enfin le nom de *Gurth* (prononcez *Gheurth*), frère du roi Harold, est orthographié avec trois lettres saxonnes : le *g*, ayant le son de *ghé* l'*y*, ayant le son d'*eu*, et le *d* barré, exprimant l'une des deux consonnances que les Anglais figurent aujourd'hui par *th*.

"Ainsi, je crois, avec la majorité des savants qui ont écrit sur la tapisserie de Bayeux, que cette tapisserie est contemporaine du grand événement qu'elle représente ; je pense, avec M. Bolton Corney, qu'elle a été exécutée sur l'ordre et aux frais du chapitre de Bayeux ; j'ajoute, pour ma part de conjectures, qu'elle fut ouvrée en Angleterre et par des mains anglaises, d'après un plan venu de Bayeux.

"Agréez, Monsieur, l'assurance de ma considération la plus distinguée.

"AUG. THIERRY.

"*Le 25 juin* 1843."

NOTE C.—*Page 25.*

In the *Northumberland Pipe Rolls,*[a] we have an interesting trace of Edgar Atheling.—He had been owing the crown 20 marks of silver, probably for the right to institute some law proceeding. Of this sum he paid 10 marks to the Sheriff of Northumberland in 1157 or 1158, and the remainder in the following year. Ten years later he paid 2 marks to the crown for the right to bring some plea. At this time he must have been about 120 years of age. He came with his father to England in 1057, as a child ; supposing him to have been 10 years of age at this period,

---

a Hodgson's Northumberland. Vol. III., Part iii., pp. 3, 11.

he would be of the great age already mentioned at the time the last payment was made. How much longer he lived there is no evidence to show. The exact place of his residence, at this time, is not known. Edlingham Castle, situated about six miles to the south-west of Alnwick, has, upon the supposition that the neighbouring village of Edlingham takes its name from him (Ætheling's ham), been by some considered to be the spot.

NOTE D.—*Page* 87.

The appearances presented on the examination of the remains of St. Cuthbert in Durham Cathedral are in consistency with the opinion that the mitre was not in vogue in Saxon times. Before the body of the saint was put in the shrine in 1104, it was inspected. Reginald, who gives us an account of the circumstance, says, " Upon the forehead of the holy bishop there is a fillet of gold, not woven work, and of gold only externally, which sparkles with most precious stones of different kinds, scattered all over its surface."[a] In 1827, when the remains were again examined, Mr. Raine tells us, " The scull of the saint was easily moved from its place ; and when this was done, we observed on the forehead, and apparently constituting a part of the bone itself, a distinct tinge of gold of the breadth of an ordinary fillet." It would thus seem that a gilded fillet was the only mitre, if such it can be called, which St. Cuthbert wore.

[a] Raine's St. Cuthbert, p 88.

FINIS.